MAD FOR
MUFFINS

MAD FOR

70 AMAZING MUFFIN RECIPES FROM SAVORY TO SWEET

MUFFINS

JEAN ANDERSON

PHOTOGRAPHS BY JASON WYCHE

Houghton Mifflin Harcourt
Boston New York 2014

For information about permission to reproduce selections from this book, write to Permissions, Houghton Mifflin Harcourt Publishing Company, 215 Park Avenue South, New York, New York 10003.

www.hmhco.com

Library of Congress Cataloging-in-Publication Data

Anderson, Jean.

   Mad for muffins : 70 amazing muffin recipes from savory to sweet / Jean Anderson.

     pages cm

   ISBN 978-0-544-22568-8 (hardback); 978-0-544-30706-3 (ebook)

1. Muffins. I. Title.

   TX770.M83A53 2014

   641.81'57—dc23

                    2014016314

Book design by Kara Plikaitis

Printed in China

C&C 10 9 8 7 6 5 4 3 2 1

Dedication

*In memory of my mother,
Marian March Johnson Anderson,
who welcomed an eager little girl into
her kitchen and taught her
how to make muffins.*

ACKNOWLEDGMENTS

First of all, profound and ongoing thanks to good friend and colleague, Joanne Lamb Hayes, for a Herculean assist in developing and testing recipes for this book. Joanne and I speak the same "recipe language," both of us having done time in the New York test kitchens of major magazines (*Ladies' Home Journal, Family Circle, Country Living*) and before that months, years even, in university food chemistry and physics labs.

Speaking of which, a salute to my long-ago Cornell professor Faith Fenton, who unraveled the mysteries of food chemistry, saw research potential in me, and made me an assistant in her own lab. Sorry to have detoured into food journalism, Dr. Fenton, but to be honest, I never had the temperament or patience to become the ace researcher that you were. You never knew how close I came to blowing up your ferociously expensive, hand-blown glass Rube Goldbergian micro-Kjeldahl unit one day while conducting protein analyses.

Huge thanks, too, to my editor, Justin Schwartz, who has both the eye of an editor and an artist. He attends every photo shoot, rare among book editors.

Finally, thanks to my savvy, persistent agent, David Black, who found the perfect home for this book. He's my rock and voice of reason in today's precarious world of book publishing.

How to Use This Book 14

Good Basic Muffins & Improvisations & Variations 32

Corn Muffins Plain & Fancy 72

Nutritious Whole-Grain Muffins 110

CONTENTS

INTRODUCTION

My mother wasn't a fancy cook but she was a good cook who baked yeast breads and rolls and muffins. Lots of muffins. For breakfast almost always and sometimes for midday dinner and supper as well.

Muffins are quick, and muffins are easy and practically foolproof if a few simple rules are followed. For these reasons, Mother taught me how to make muffins before moving on to more complex cakes and cookies. I couldn't have been more than four at the time, at least I know that I hadn't learned to read well enough to follow a recipe.

I remember those early lessons well and in particular the reason why muffins are so quick, so easy: Dry ingredients combined in one bowl, wets in a second, then the two mixed—but barely. This is key if muffins are to be fine and feathery. The wets and drys should be mixed only enough to combine; in fact muffin batters should be lumpy with flecks of flour clearly visible. If not, your muffins will be peaked and rubbery and riddled with tunnels.

I began with a no-nonsense muffin, no frills, what I call Entry-Level Muffins (page 34), then proceeded to Date Muffins (page 36), equally easy except for pitting the sticky dates and snipping them into little pieces (oh, for the pre-snipped dates every supermarket now sells).

With Mother there to coach me, I learned to sift and measure flour in the proper dry measuring cups (we called these little nested cups "Mary Annes"). I loved the way they stacked: the ¼ cup measure tucked into the ⅓ cup, those two tucked into the ½ cup, then all three neatly housed in the 1 cup measure.

I learned, too, that spouted glass measures were for liquids—milk, vegetable oils, molasses, syrups, fruit juices, and such. And even more important, that they should never be used for flours, sugars, meals, and other dry ingredients because it is impossible to measure them accurately—no filling to the top, then scooping off the excess as I had learned to do with the Mary Annes.

Muffins launched me into the world of baking and I'd barely soloed before I was improvising with the basic recipes I now considered boring. My itch to improvise has never waned, in fact my reason for writing *MAD FOR MUFFINS* was to create a portfolio of muffins that captured the unusual, often seductive flavors I'd discovered as a food and travel writer constantly on assignment—in Europe, Africa, Asia, the Middle East, South America.

So why not the curries and chutneys of India captured in a muffin?

The lemongrass of Thailand? The coconut milk of half a dozen Asian countries? The falafel and hummus of the Middle East? The sun-dried tomatoes, pepperoni, and exquisite cheeses of Italy?

And how could I neglect the peppery accents of our own Southwest . . . the whole-wheats and ryes, other grains and brans of the prairie states . . . the silken stone-ground cornmeals of the South, to say nothing of its twenty-four-karat sweet potatoes . . . the maple sugars and syrups of New England as well as its cranberries now available dried as well as fresh and frozen? Oh, yes, and the sharp Cheddars of Vermont and Wisconsin, not to mention the country hams of Kentucky, Tennessee, and Virginia.

My mission, too, was to reduce whenever possible, as much as possible, the amount of sugar now integral to so many of today's muffins. Have you noticed that "muffin" has become a euphemism for "cupcake"? Do we really feel less guilty scarfing down a sugary muffin than a cupcake? Well, as one friend commented, "At least muffins aren't frosted!" True, but they may be strewn with a buttery, sugary topping.

To sate America's sweet tooth, I've added a chapter of "party pleasers," a collection of—dare I call them—"dessert" muffins? Just the thing for birthday parties, showers, and other celebrations.

No, I haven't forsaken basic muffin recipes in the pages that follow nor ignored the fruit-nut muffins handed down from our grand-mothers. They're all here—in abundance—though perhaps a tad less sweet. Here, too, the tips and techniques you'll need to produce proper muffins.

So, I hope you'll give my muffins a try—the plain, the fancy, the familiar, the exotic.

Jean Anderson, Chapel Hill, NC

How to Use This BOOK

About Muffins

THE MUFFIN METHOD is one of the four basic methods of mixing every beginner learns, the other three being the Pastry Method, the Butter Cake Method, and the Sponge or Angel Cake Method. The Muffin Method's the simplest, in fact it's as easy as one, two, three.

1 COMBINE all dry ingredients (flour and/or cornmeal or other grain; sugar, baking powder and/or soda; salt, and any dry seasonings) in a large bowl, add any chopped nuts or dried fruits or grated cheese, toss to mix, and then make a well in the middle of the dry ingredients.

2 WHISK all liquids (milk or other liquid; melted butter, oil, or other shortening; and egg plus any liquid flavorings) together in a small bowl until frothy.

3 POUR the combined liquids into the well in the dry ingredients and stir only enough to combine—the batter should be lumpy with flecks of flour clearly visible.

That's all there is to it and yet step three is the most critical, the most difficult to master. We tend to think that all batters must be satin-smooth, that every speck of flour must be incorporated. Dead wrong if you're making muffins.

My mother stood over me as I mixed my first batch of muffins and scientist that she was, had me divide the batter in half, leaving one half lumpy and flecked with flour and the second half beaten until smooth.

We baked the two batches in separate pans so that I could see the difference between properly and improperly mixed muffins. It could not have been more dramatic. The "good" muffins were delicately rounded on top, lightly browned, and when broken open, fine and feathery throughout.

But the batter I'd beaten to death? Those muffins had Alpine peaks, felt tough when I eased them from the pan, and even worse, were cratered inside, pocked with tunnels that angled up from the bottom into those lofty peaks. And yes, these muffins were rubbery, not worth eating. We fed them to the birds.

From that day forward, I've always slightly under-mixed my muffin batters, the lesson every successful muffin maker learns. I can still hear my mother saying, "Don't worry about the lumps in the batter, Jean. Don't worry about those specks of flour. They will magically disappear as the muffins bake."

And so they do.

About Reheating Muffins

Because I've trimmed the sugar in many of the muffin recipes that follow as well as the amount of fat, leftovers may dry somewhat on standing (sugar, few people realize, absorbs atmospheric moisture). The best plan is to freeze any leftover muffins, then reheat as needed. First of all, forget about reheating frozen muffins by microwave; they will be tough. And do not reheat more than four standard-size muffins at a time because they'll heat unevenly.

Arrange still-frozen muffin(s) on a sheet of heavy-duty foil, side by side if two, in a triangle if three with muffins equidistant from one another, and in a circle if four, again with the muffins equidistant.

Bring ends of foil up, then roll down and seal bundle hobo-style.

Slide onto the middle shelf of a preheated 350°F oven and leave until an instant-read thermometer, inserted into the middle of a muffin, registers at least 125°F.

So how long does this take? Here's an approximate timetable:

1 standard-size muffin: 10 minutes

2 standard-size muffins: 15 minutes

3 standard-size muffins: 18 minutes

4 standard-size muffins: 20 minutes

NOTE: *Two jumbo-size muffins (the most you should reheat at a time) take 25 minutes. And "minis"? We arranged six in two rows of three and they were ready to eat in 10 minutes.*

Recipe Basics (Getting Started, Etc.)

NOTE: *Before beginning any muffin recipe, please review this section carefully. It discusses muffin pans, ingredients, techniques, and other helpful basics.*

Read each recipe carefully—several times or until you know exactly what you're to do as well as what implements and ingredients you'll need.

To save time, measure all recipe ingredients at the outset and do as much advance prep as possible (peeling, coring, slicing, etc.) so there's no need to pause and search mid-recipe. Also have all pans and implements at the ready.

Do not substitute one ingredient for another unless substitutions are suggested.

The best muffin pans are top-quality aluminum because they conduct heat more effectively than stainless steel pans. I don't like nonstick pans and avoid darkly coated ones because muffins baked in them tend to overbrown and may even burn on the bottom.

Allow 20 minutes for an oven to preheat to the temperature you've set.

Keep a reliable oven thermometer in your oven, placing it where the manufacturer recommends, and check it often to determine whether your oven is accurate. Most home ovens run high or low—often by as much as fifty degrees, which of course can ruin a recipe. In some areas, utility companies will calibrate your oven for you or can recommend someone who will.

Note that all muffin baking times given in this book are for standard ovens—not convection ovens, which bake faster because of fans circulating the hot air. If you have a convection oven, consult the owner's manual. Many will suggest baking time adjustments. If not, try reducing muffin baking times by 10 minutes, then if muffins are not done (a toothpick inserted in the center of one should come out clean), continue baking and testing in 3- or 4-minute intervals. Once you've determined the difference in baking times, make a note of it and keep that note handy.

Ingredients

Bacon: Crumbled, crisply cooked bacon makes a fine addition to muffins (see Bacon 'n' Eggs Breakfast Muffins (page 48), also Easy Add-Ons for Chili-Cheddar Two-Corn Muffins (page 88). Fortunately, many artisanal bacons—slab (one piece) and sliced thick or thin—are now available in specialty groceries as well as online. I only use the nitrite-free and suggest that you do the same. See Sources (page 220).

Bacon Drippings: Being a frugal cook, my mother kept a half-pint preserving jar of bacon drippings in her refrigerator not only for seasoning leafy green vegetables but also as the fat in a variety of muffins. I, myself, like drippings best in corn breads. If you're concerned about the calories and cholesterol in bacon drippings, let me just say that pork fat is less saturated than butter or vegetable shortening.

Benne (Sesame) Seeds: Considered good luck by the slaves who brought pockets full of these little African seeds into the South during the seventeenth and eighteenth centuries, benne remain popular to this day in and around Charleston, South Carolina, where they're baked into biscuits, cookies, and cocktail snacks. If lightly toasted, they're equally delicious in muffins (see Toasted Benne Seed Muffins, page 52). **Tip:** Being oily, sesame seeds quickly stale and go rancid, so buy only a small jar at a time and once open, store on the refrigerator door shelf.

HOW TO TOAST SESAME SEEDS

Spread in a 9-inch aluminum pie pan (not a darkly coated one, which will hasten the browning), slide onto the middle shelf of a preheated 275°F oven, and leave until pale golden and intensely aromatic—4 to 5 minutes. Cool to room temperature before using.

Black Pepper: Believe it or not, a pinch or two of black pepper improves the flavor of almost any muffin. Freshly ground black pepper, that is, so keep your peppermill loaded. **Tip:** 10 energetic grinds of the peppermill = about $\frac{1}{4}$ teaspoon freshly ground black pepper, 20 grinds approximately $\frac{1}{2}$ teaspoon.

Black Walnuts: An American original, this cousin of the hickory nut encased in a rock-hard shell is the very devil to extract. Fortunately, black walnut meats can be ordered online; see Sources (page 220). Their flavor is unique, a bit sweet, a bit meaty, even—dare I say a bit musky?—utterly unlike the more familiar English walnuts.

Bran: The nutrient- and fiber-rich husk or outer layer of oats, rye, wheat, and other grains. Whole-grain flours contain bran, refined ones do not. A stroll down the cereal aisle of any supermarket is to see dozens of bran cereals, the majority of them wheat bran cereals—bran flakes, buds, or All-Bran, in my opinion the best choice for Classic Bran Muffins (page 126) and any variations.

Butter: All recipes in this book were developed and tested with old-fashioned stick butter (mainly unsalted), so do not use soft butter, whipped butter, faux butter, margarine, or vegetable shortening. The majority also call for melted butter, so I slice what I need from a stick of butter, drop into a spouted 1-quart oven-proof glass measuring cup, and microwave uncovered on Defrost. In my 650-watt oven, it takes about 5 minutes on Defrost to melt ¼ cup (½ stick) butter. Of course, times vary according to the microwave's wattage as well as the amount of butter being melted. Try 5 minutes on Defrost, then continue microwaving in 1- or 2-minute increments until your butter is liquid gold. You'll soon learn what works best in your particular microwave oven.

Buttermilk: Many of my muffins—especially the corn muffins—are made with buttermilk. Use regular buttermilk, not fat-free, unless recipes direct otherwise.

Cheddar, Jack & Other Semi-Hard Cheeses: The cheeses I use in muffins are freshly grated—always—because the packaged, pregrated seems drier, doesn't melt smoothly, and isn't very flavorful. Several of my recipes call for Vermont Cheddar, which can be ordered online (see Sources, page 220). For grating small amounts of cheese, a coarse-toothed Microplane is perfect; for larger ones, the food processor shredding disk. To save time, I keep these ballpark equivalents handy:

2 ounces cheese = ½ cup grated

4 ounces cheese (¼ pound) = 1 cup grated

8 ounces cheese (½ pound) = 2 cups grated

12 ounces cheese (¾ pound) = 3 cups grated

16 ounces (1 pound) = 4 cups grated

Also see Parmigiano-Reggiano (page 26).

Chocolate Hazelnut Spread: Oh, my, what delicious stuff. In the beginning there was Nutella, now other brands are out there as well and this spread is challenging peanut butter as this nation's favorite sandwich spread. And like peanut butter, it can become an ingredient in all manner of baked goods. See Toasted Hazelnut Muffins (page 145).

Citrus Juices: Whenever a muffin calls for orange, lemon, or other citrus juice, squeeze the amounts you need. In a pinch, reconstituted frozen juice may be okay but it doesn't have the flavor of freshly squeezed juice.

Citrus Zest: The best way to boost the fresh orange or lemon flavor of a muffin (or any recipe, for that matter) is to add a little finely grated zest (colored part of the rind). With a moderately fine-toothed Microplane, the job's done zip-quick because you'll rarely need more than a teaspoon or two.

Cocoa Powder: Cocoa is a better choice for muffins than chocolate because it can be mixed with the dry ingredients. Not so chocolate, which must be melted, then combined with the liquids, and only then stirred into the drys. Any good brand of cocoa will do as long as it's unsweetened.

Coconut: If I'm going to make coconut cakes, cookies, or pies, I'll go to all the trouble of wrestling with a fresh coconut, cracking the shell, draining off the liquid, breaking up the chunks inside, peeling off the brown skin, then grating the snowy flesh on a four-sided grater. Talk about labor intensive. But for the small amount of coconut I might use in a muffin recipe, I admit to using packaged, preshredded or flaked coconut though I do try to use the unsweetened.

Coconut Milk: Thanks to the proliferation of Thai restaurants in this country, coconut milk has come to the supermarket. So in developing new recipes for this book, I decided to see if coconut milk could be substituted for regular milk in certain muffin recipes. Indeed, it can (see Not Your Mama's Carrot Muffins, page 121). You can buy pure coconut milk (unsweetened)—organic or otherwise. You can buy regular (my preference), "lite," or reduced-fat coconut milk. Look for them in the international section of your supermarket or specialty grocery in handy 13.5- to 14-ounce cans.

Coffee, Espresso: Mocha (chocolate + coffee) is a particular flavor favorite of mine and when making muffins, the most effective way to combine the two is by using unsweetened cocoa powder and instant espresso powder or crystals.

Cornmeal: Basically, there are two types of cornmeal: stone-ground cornmeal (either white, the Southerner's choice, or yellow) and the big brand granular yellow cornmeal most supermarkets carry. Stone-ground meal is floury, more flavorful, and nutritionally superior because it usually contains both husk and germ. The downside is that its shelf life is short, so it should be stored in an airtight container in the refrigerator or freezer. Like whole-wheat flour, stone-ground cornmeal is usually not sifted before it's measured—my recipes all specify. If your supermarket does not sell stone-ground cornmeal, you can order it online (see Sources, page 220).

Corn Powder, Freeze-Dried: I recently discovered this new corn product and decided to give it a try. It's said to boost the corn flavor in whatever it's used in, indeed to inject something approaching dried corn flavor. (See Full-of-Flavor Corn Muffins, page 77. Also see Sources, page 220.)

Country Ham & Smithfield Ham: Unlike the popular pink packing-house hams every supermarket sells, country hams are firmer (no injected water), saltier, deeply flavorful, and the color of mahogany. Three of this country's finest are the Edwards Hams of Virginia, Benton's Smoky Mountain Country Hams of Tennessee, and Col. Newsom's Aged Kentucky Country Hams; all are available online (see Sources, page 220). Some country hams are sold by the ounce as well as fully cooked and ready to use and that's what you want. Most muffin recipes call for only a few ounces, so no leftovers. If you must buy a larger amount of country ham, simply freeze the excess and use later in any recipes calling for ham. **Tip:** If country ham is unavailable, prosciutto and Serrano ham, either imported or domestic, make good substitutes.

Cracklin's: The crispy bits left after lard is rendered. Prizing both their texture and meaty flavor, Southerners stir them into corn bread. See Corn Muffins with Cracklin's (page 78).

Dried Fruits: When I was growing up, the only dried fruits local groceries sold were apricots, dates, and raisins. Today the supermarket inventory of dried fruits is vast: apples, apricots, blueberries, cranberries, currants (actually Zante raisins), dates (now pitted, diced, and ready to use), figs, peaches, pears, dark seedless raisins, and sultanas (golden raisins). Dried apples, apricots, pears, and peaches may have been sulfured to minimize browning, but I prefer the unsulfured. Dried fruits mean that you can enjoy blueberry muffins right around the calendar, ditto cranberry muffins and peach muffins. Even if peaches, apples, or pears are in season, adding some of the dried, coarsely chopped, boosts the fruit flavor.

Eggs: Unless recipes in this book specify otherwise, use large eggs. Believe it or not, some of my muffins contain chopped hard-cooked eggs and I'd like to share here my foolproof way of hard-cooking them:

HOW TO HARD-COOK EGGS

Bring eggs to a boil over moderate heat in a medium-size saucepan with enough cold water to cover them by a couple of inches. As soon as the water boils, set pan off-heat, cover, and let eggs stand 15 minutes exactly. Drain the eggs and plunge into ice water—this prevents that ugly dark green ring from forming between the yolks and whites. Tip: Eggs near their sell-by date peel much more easily and neatly than fresh ones. I crack the broad end first, roll the egg on the counter to craze the shell, then thumb bits of it off under a slow stream of cold water. I also do one egg at a time because if a cracked and crazed egg is returned to the pan of cold water, it will be difficult to shell without tearing or gouging the white.

Evaporated Milk: I've always liked the slightly caramel flavor of evaporated milk and for that reason, call for it in several muffin recipes. Note: I'm talking evaporated milk here, not sweetened condensed, and the one I prefer is regular, not low-fat or fat-free.

Flour: Throughout this book, I call for *sifted* all-purpose flour meaning that you should sift the flour before you measure it even if the package says "presifted." Flour compacts when shipped or stored, so if you merely spoon it from bag to measuring cup, your 1 cup flour may actually be 1⅓ cups or—horrors—1½ cups. Enough to ruin any muffin. So sift, then measure.

Hazelnuts: Often overlooked, these brown-skinned chickpea-size nuts are becoming more widely available and, as I discovered while developing recipes for

this book, are perfectly delicious in muffins and can be substituted for pecans or walnuts. But they must be toasted.

HOW TO TOAST HAZELNUTS

Spread shelled hazelnuts on an ungreased rimmed baking sheet, slide onto middle shelf of a preheated 350°F oven, and leave until skins begin to blister and the nuts smell irresistible—10 to 12 minutes. Bundle hot nuts in a clean, dry dish towel and rub energetically to slake off skins. Don't worry about any recalcitrant bits clinging to the nuts. They'll add color and texture.

Herbs: With fresh herbs as near as the nearest supermarket or farmer's market, I urge you to use them in muffins because their flavor is superior to that of dried herbs—dried leaf herbs, not ground. The herbs I like best in muffins? Parsley, of course, but also chives, dill, thyme, marjoram, oregano, and occasionally stronger herbs like sage and rosemary. But wherever I call for fresh herbs, I also give the dried herb equivalent. As a rule, 1 tablespoon freshly chopped herb = 1 teaspoon crumbled dried herb, though for unusually pungent herbs—rosemary and sage, to name two—I substitute ½ to ¾ teaspoon crumbled dried herb for each tablespoon of freshly chopped.

Hickory Nuts: Though first cousins to pecans, wild hickory nuts are hard shelled and their meat takes hours to extract. I remember my father spending an entire evening shelling a bowl of nuts that the tall hickory in front of our house rained down upon us like hailstones each fall. He considered that time well spent because wild hickory nuts are so flavorful and rich. Fortunately, you can order shelled, ready-to-use wild hickory nuts online. See Sources (page 220).

Honey: When a recipe calls for honey—and a few of my muffin recipes do—use a light golden honey the consistency of corn syrup. Never substitute honey for sugar in any muffin recipe because you are courting disaster, a lesson I learned the hard way. The properties and chemical compositions of these two sweeteners are entirely different and honey, always unpredictable when used in baked goods, works only in recipes developed specifically for it.

Maple Extract: Only use pure maple extract, never artificial, which tastes, well, artificial. Moreover, only pure maple extract has the assertiveness to impart maple flavor to muffins, or to any baked good, for that matter. Some high-end groceries carry pure maple extract but few supermarkets do. Fortunately, pure maple extract can be ordered online (see Sources, page 220).

Maple Sugar, Granulated: Most of us know maple sugar as little candies shaped like maple leaves, but when it comes to baking, you need granulated maple sugar. It looks a little like raw sugar but tastes purely of maple. A few high-end groceries carry it, but it's more widely available online in amounts as small as 4 ounces and as whopping as 40 pounds (see Sources, page 220).

Maple Syrup: As a rule, it takes 40 to 50 gallons of maple sap to make 1 gallon of maple syrup. In Canada, maple syrup must be at least 66 percent sugar and in the U.S., it cannot be labeled "maple syrup" unless made exclusively from maple sap. There are several grades of maple syrup (from Fancy through A to B). But, make a note, grade has nothing to do with quality. It has to do with color and flavor. Grade A syrup is golden and delicately flavored,

perfect for pancakes and waffles. But for baking, Grade B is what you want because its flavor is intense. Some high-end groceries sell Grade B maple syrup and it's widely available online (see Sources, page 220). Whatever you use, make sure it's labeled "pure maple syrup."

Masa Harina: Every now and then I'll substitute a little of this "tortilla flour" for cornmeal in corn muffins because it imparts subtle New Mexico (or old Mexico) flavor (see Mexicali Muffins, page 106). And what, exactly, is tortilla flour? Finely ground dried hominy. And what exactly is hominy? Fresh corn kernels soaked in a lye bath till they puff and their skins pop off. Called "posole" in Mexico whether dried or soft, it's integral to many south-of-the-border classics. Soft hominy is also popular in the American South where it's known as "big hominy." But only when the hominy is dried and ground does it become masa harina. Today many supermarkets carry it and every Latino grocery definitely does. Still, if you can't find small bags of masa harina, try ordering it online (see Sources, page 220).

Molasses: Several of my recipes call for molasses that's not too dark, meaning unsulfured molasses the consistency of corn syrup. Under no circumstances use blackstrap molasses.

Nutmeg: Once you've tasted the spicy-lemony flavor of freshly grated nutmeg, you're not likely to settle for preground nutmeg. Thanks to today's Microplanes, whole nutmegs can be grated zip-quick. Moreover, they don't lose flavor the way preground nutmeg does.

Oatmeal: Called "rolled oats" in recipes. Sometimes I call for quick-cooking rolled oats but if I'm after a bit more crunch, I'll specify old-fashioned rolled oats. To be honest, however, the two can be used interchangeably, so suit yourself.

Oil: Whenever one of my muffin recipes calls for oil, use the one I specify—maybe vegetable oil (just a pale golden blend), peanut oil, corn oil, even extra-virgin olive oil (see Polenta Muffins with Parmigiano-Reggiano and Rosemary, page 97, and Butternut–Pine Nut Muffins, page 158).

Parmigiano-Reggiano: This famous cheese from the north of Italy is blessed with the perfect balance of flavors—sweet/salty/nutty. To inject cheese flavor in a muffin, a little freshly grated Parmigiano-Reggiano does the trick. I won't pretend that this imported cheese is as cheap as Cheddar. It isn't. But you can save money if you buy it by the chunk and grate it in your food processor—30 seconds is all it takes. Stored in the refrigerator in a tightly capped 1-pint preserving jar, it will remain fresh for as long as a month.

Peanut Butter: For muffins, I prefer chunky peanut butter to creamy not only because it adds texture but also because its flavor is more pronounced (see PB & J Muffins, page 62).

Peanuts: Highly nutritious legumes that mature underground, peanuts are good sources of protein, niacin and folate (two B vitamins), vitamin E, and three major minerals (magnesium, manganese, and phosphorus). Yet peanuts contain no cholesterol, no sodium, and no trans-fats, their oils being largely unsaturated. Adding peanuts to muffins, especially unsalted dry-roasted peanuts, is a good way to boost their food value (see Not Your Mama's Carrot Muffins, page 121).

Pecans: A valuable food source among Native Americans long before Columbus, the pecan has become the all-American nut. We bake pecans into cookies, cakes, quick loaves, pies, and yes, muffins. Like other nuts, pecans are a nutritious, far better snack food than chips or cookies. Moreover, they contain significant amounts of largely unsaturated oleic acid (thought to lower LDL, or "bad cholesterol") as well as phytochemicals now believed to reduce the risk of heart disease as well as colon and stomach cancer. Because I insist upon pecans that are sweet and fresh (never true of the canned or prepackaged), I order new-crop pecans directly from the grower (see Sources, page 220).

HOW TO TOAST PECANS

Spread pecans on an ungreased rimmed baking sheet, slide onto middle shelf of a preheated 350°F oven, and leave until nuts smell irresistible—7 to 8 minutes. Watch closely—nuts burn fast. Don't chop the pecans till they're toasted.

Persimmons: American persimmon trees grow wild across the South and Midwest and between late September and mid-December bear intensely flavored fruits no bigger than Ping-Pong balls. Shriveled windfalls—orange with a haze

of mauve—are what gleaners seek. Ditto deer, possums, and raccoons who devour them almost as fast as they drop from the trees.

HOW TO PUREE PERSIMMONS

Rinse persimmons three times in cold water, drain on paper toweling, and pat dry. Now push persimmons through a food mill set over a large nonreactive bowl. Discard solids. Yield: 1 quart wild persimmons = about 1 pint (2 cups) puree.

HOW TO FREEZE PERSIMMON PUREE

Mix ⅛ teaspoon powdered ascorbic acid (vitamin C) with each 1 quart persimmon puree (this prevents browning). Pack puree in 1-pint freezer containers leaving ½-inch head space at top. Snap on lids, date, label, and set in 0°F freezer. Use in any recipe that calls for unsweetened persimmon puree or pulp. Storage time: about 1 year.

NOTE: *Frozen wild persimmon puree is also available online but supplies are short, especially in spring and summer (see Sources, page 220).*

Pignoli (Pine Nuts): The first time I toasted these buttery nuts that taste of pine resin, I was in Santa Fe, New Mexico, not Italy. Called piñon nuts in this part of the world, these seeds of the stubby piñon pine have sustained the Pueblo Indians for centuries and for that reason are highly prized. Today pine nuts are baked into all manner of breads, shortbreads, and cookies. Stirred into brittles and fudges, too. I like to snack on them both raw and toasted. And of course, like them in muffins.

HOW TO TOAST PIGNOLI (PINE NUTS)

Because these nuts are ultra-rich, they brown quickly and for that reason I don't go the skillet route where the inevitable hot spots might burn them. Instead, I spread the whole shelled nuts in a bright aluminum or stainless steel 9-inch pie pan, slide onto the middle shelf of a preheated 350°F oven, and toast, shaking the pan well a time or two, until the color of pale caramel— 3 to 5 minutes. But keep an eye on them—pine nuts burn easily. Cool the toasted nuts until easy to handle, then give them a coarse chop— just enough to halve or quarter them.

Rye Flour: There are many different types of rye flour—light, medium, dark, whole-grain, and pumpernickel. Dark rye flour works best for muffins, I think, because of its color and flavor. Do not sift it before measuring, in fact do not sift it, period. Bits of husk and germ add texture and nutritive value. Rye muffins also need wheat flour because its stronger gluten builds the framework of almost all breads. A fifty-fifty ratio—rye flour to all-purpose flour—makes perfect muffins though my Brown Bread Muffins (page 133) call for equal parts dark rye flour, all-purpose flour, and cornmeal. To buy rye flour online, see Sources (page 220).

Salt: For all-round baking, I prefer uniodized table salt. I personally find kosher or coarse salt too grainy for muffins because it doesn't always dissolve in the short period of time it takes to bake a muffin.

Sour Cream: For some reason 8-ounce cartons of sour cream are disappearing from supermarket shelves in some parts of the country. Not to worry. Simply pack sour cream into a 1-cup measure—the kind used for measuring flour—and level off the top with the broad side of a small spatula. **Note:** Unless I suggest "light" or low-fat sour cream for a particular recipe, do not use it.

Soy Flour: This fine powder ground from toasted soybeans is protein- and mineral-rich, and the natural, full-fat soy flour, when combined with all-purpose flour, makes muffins as delicious as they are nutritious (see Soy Flour Muffins with Dried Blueberries and Cranberries, page 166). Most upmarket groceries now sell soy flour and it can also be ordered online (see Sources, page 220).

Sugar: Unless otherwise specified, the sugar used in my muffin recipes is granulated sugar, but whenever two different sugars are used in a single recipe—granulated and light brown for example—each one is specified. Many of my muffins call for raw sugar (also known as turbinado), a pale brown granulated sugar that tastes more of caramel than of molasses.

Sweet Potatoes: The potatoes Columbus took back to Spain were sweet potatoes, not Irish potatoes. And nowhere are they more popular today than in the American South. North Carolina produces more sweet potatoes than any other state, with Louisiana raising its share. Of all the varieties available, the two I like best are the intensely orange Beauregards and the plumper, rounder, copper-hued Jewels.

Neither is difficult to find. Whenever I need mashed sweet potatoes for a recipe, I bake them because baking intensifies the flavor and doesn't water down the flesh. Moreover, nothing could be easier:

HOW TO BAKE, MEASURE, AND MASH SWEET POTATOES

Prick potatoes with a kitchen fork, place in pie pan, slide onto middle shelf of a preheated 400°F oven, and bake about 1 hour or until soft enough to pierce easily with a fork or skewer.

Remove potatoes from the oven, cool until easy to handle, then cut an X in the top of each, and pinch to push flesh up.

Scoop flesh into a bowl and using a potato masher, mash until smooth or into a silky puree—whichever the recipe specifies.

To measure, scoop pureed or mashed sweet potato into a dry measure (the kind used for flour and sugar), packing or not as recipes specify, then level off top with broad side of a small spatula. For 1 cup firmly packed pureed or mashed sweet potato you'll need 1 large potato (about 10 ounces).

Cool pureed or mashed sweet potato before using and do not season unless recipes direct otherwise.

Vanilla and Other Extracts: Always use pure extracts, never imitation, which are disagreeably perfume-y and rarely taste like the real thing. A faux extract can ruin a perfectly good muffin.

Whole-Wheat Flour: Unlike all-purpose flour milled exclusively from the starchy endosperm, whole-wheat flour contains the husk, germ, and endosperm. It's protein-rich, fiber-rich, and an impressive source of such major B vitamins as thiamine, riboflavin, niacin, B_6, folate, and pantothenic acid. In addition, whole-wheat flour contains a mother lode of minerals (iron, manganese, magnesium, phosphorus, potassium, and selenium). But it's too heavy to make a good muffin unless lightened with all-purpose flour. The usual ratio is 50 percent whole-wheat and 50 percent all-purpose though amounts may vary somewhat from recipe to recipe. Most good supermarkets routinely carry whole-wheat flours and high-end groceries invariably do. There are online sources as well (see Sources, page 220).

Measuring Tips

Ice Cream Scoop: The $1/4$-cup size is just the thing for filling muffin pan cups, especially a spring-loaded one that scrapes every bit of batter from scoop to pan. One scoop is about right for one standard-size muffin pan cup, more scoops, of course, for muffin tops and jumbos. For mini muffins, I use a teaspoon or tablespoon, adding enough batter to two-thirds fill each muffin pan cup—no more.

Measuring Cups: There are two basic types of measuring cups, one for liquids, the second for dry or soft, thick ingredients. Here are the correct ways to use them.

Spouted Measuring Cups

For Liquids: Broths . . . fruit and vegetable juices . . . milk and cream . . . oils and vinegars . . . honey, molasses, and syrups . . . water . . . beers, wines, and spirits.

Technique: Set measuring cup on a flat surface and fill to desired amount ($1/4$ cup, $1/2$ cup, 1 cup, etc.), then bend down and confirm amount at eye level.

"Dry" Measures (¼-, ⅓-, ½-, and 1-Cup Sizes)

Technique: For the following ingredients, spoon ingredient into measuring cup of desired size, packing as you go, and level off the top with the broad side of a small spatula: brown sugar (light or dark) . . . butter, lard, shortening . . . chutneys, relishes . . . cream cheese, cheese spreads . . . fruit and vegetable purees, applesauce, mashed Irish or sweet potatoes . . . jams, jellies, marmalades, and preserves . . . ketchup, chili sauce, tomato paste, bottled pasta sauces . . . lard, soft butter or margarine, vegetable shortening . . . mayonnaise, mustard . . . peanut butter, Nutella, tahini, other nut and seed pastes . . . sour cream, yogurt.

Technique: For these ingredients, simply spoon into measuring cup and level off with the edge of a small spatula: bread and cracker crumbs . . . bran flakes or buds, uncooked oatmeal (rolled oats) and other grains . . . grated or shredded cheeses . . . cornmeal (stone-ground or granular) . . . dried fruits (raisins, currants, chopped dried blueberries, cranberries, dates, etc.) . . . flours (all-purpose, cake, whole-wheat, rice, rye, etc.) . . . fresh fruits (chopped, diced, sliced) . . . fresh herbs (chopped, minced, snipped) . . . chopped or grated fresh ginger . . . nuts (halves, pieces, chopped) . . . sugar (granulated, raw, confectioners') . . . vegetables (chopped, diced, or sliced).

Some Handy Equivalents

In the old days, muffin pans were more or less the same size. Not so today when in addition to standard-size muffin pans there are minis; jumbos; even broader, shallower muffin top pans for those whose favorite part of a muffin is the crunchy, often caramelized top. So here's a handy table of equivalents based upon a recipe that makes a dozen standard-size muffins:

12 standard-size muffins =
about 3 dozen (36) mini muffins

12 standard-size muffins =
10 to 12 muffin tops

12 standard-size muffins =
5 to 6 jumbo muffins

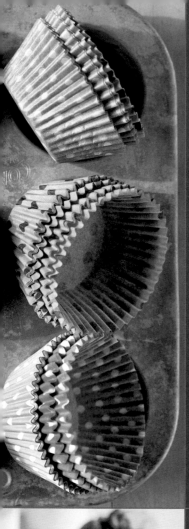

Good Basic
MUFFINS
&
Improvisations
& Variations

Ever since I was a little girl, muffins invited "improv," but in the beginning disaster followed disaster. All because I hadn't mastered the hard-and-fast rules of successful muffin-making:

o Never stray too far from the basic recipe my mother taught me: 2 cups sifted flour . . . 2 tablespoons sugar . . . 1 tablespoon baking powder . . . 1 teaspoon salt . . . 1 cup milk . . . 1 large egg . . . 3 tablespoons vegetable oil or melted butter.

o Use only the muffin method of mixing: Combine all dry ingredients in a mixing bowl and make a well in the center, then whisk all liquids together in a small bowl, pour into the well in the dry ingredients, and *stir only enough to combine.* The batter should be lumpy with flecks of flour clearly visible. This is key.

o Spoon batter into prepared muffin pan cups (greased or spritzed with nonstick cooking spray or lined with crinkly paper cups), approximately two-thirds filling each cup.

o Bake on the middle shelf of a hot oven—usually 400°F to 425°F—just until a toothpick inserted in the center of a muffin comes out clean—20 to 25 minutes. Richer muffins, I later learned, require somewhat lower oven temperatures—say 375°F—if they are to bake without over-browning or burning.

o Serve hot with unsalted butter, jam, or jelly. Or drizzle with honey.

Only after repeated doses of food chemistry at Cornell did I learn to improvise on the basic muffin recipe without mishap, how to compensate for more sugar (or less), more fat (or less), the addition of something wet (like shredded zucchini) as well as how to substitute other liquids for milk, other fats for oil or butter. The recipes that follow are some of my favorite improvisations. The lion's share were created specifically for this cookbook.

Entry-Level Muffins

**makes about
1 dozen**

I call these "entry-level" muffins because this is the recipe to try if you've never made a muffin. It's a basic recipe, the *classic* muffin recipe, the one most of us try first. I couldn't have been more than four when my mother invited me into her kitchen one day, showed me how to sift flour, how to crack an egg, how to measure ingredients both liquid and dry. She showed me how to set the oven temperature and how to grease muffin pans, then said, "Let's make muffins." Her mantra: "Don't over-mix, don't overmix, don't overmix." I remember that that first muffin batter was lumpy, that there were flecks of flour everywhere. But what I remember most of all was Mother's saying, "Don't worry, Jean. The lumps and bits of flour will vanish as the muffins bake." And as if by magic, they did!

2 cups sifted all-purpose
flour

2 tablespoons sugar

1 tablespoon baking
powder

1 teaspoon salt

1 cup milk

3 tablespoons vegetable
oil or melted unsalted
butter

1 large egg, well beaten

1 Preheat oven to 425°F. Lightly grease 12 standard-size muffin pan cups or spritz with nonstick cooking spray or, if you prefer, insert a crinkly muffin liner into each cup. Set pans aside.

2 Combine flour, sugar, baking powder, and salt in medium mixing bowl, make well in center of dry ingredients, and set aside.

3 Whisk milk with oil and egg in small bowl until smooth, pour into well in dry ingredients, and stir only enough to combine—batter should be lumpy and specks of flour clearly visible.

4 Spoon batter into muffin pans, dividing amount equally—
   each muffin pan cup will be approximately two-thirds full,
   though occasionally a bit more or a bit less.

5 Slide onto middle oven shelf and bake about 20 minutes
   until muffins have risen and their tops are nicely rounded
   and evenly browned.

6 Serve hot with plenty of unsalted butter.

**EASY ADD-ONS (TOSS WITH DRY INGREDIENTS
BEFORE ADDING COMBINED LIQUIDS):**

* $\frac{1}{4}$ cup crumbled crisply cooked bacon

* $\frac{1}{2}$ cup dark seedless raisins or dried currants

* $\frac{1}{2}$ cup dried blueberries

* $\frac{1}{2}$ cup coarsely chopped pecans or walnuts

VARIATION:

Muffins All Children Love: Prepare the basic recipe—as is
or with one of the Easy Add-Ons—bake, then the instant the
muffins are done, dip the tops in melted unsalted butter ($\frac{1}{4}$ cup
or $\frac{1}{2}$ stick is about right), then in $\frac{1}{3}$ cup Cinnamon-Sugar (page
217) until nicely coated. Makes about 1 dozen.

Date Muffins

makes about
1 dozen

Once you've mastered Entry-Level Muffins (page 34), you should have no trouble making all kinds of muffins. These are the ones my mother taught me to bake after she pronounced my "entry-level" muffins perfect. Once again my mother cautioned me, "Don't overmix, don't overmix, don't overmix," advice that applies to almost every muffin you will make. The notable exception? Muffins mixed by the butter cake method (see Sally Lunn Muffins, page 175) **Note:** *Today, thank heavens, we can buy prepitted, prediced dates. Not so when I was a child, so to make the job less "sticky," my mother showed me how to grease the scissor blades—ever so carefully—so the dates wouldn't stick as I snipped them into small pieces. Something to remember if you can't find ready-to-use date pieces (today's nonstick cooking spray is even more effective).*

VARIATIONS:

Date-Nut Muffins: Prepare as directed using ⅓ cup each finely diced pitted dates and moderately finely chopped pecans, walnuts, or black walnuts instead of ¾ cup dates. Makes about 1 dozen.

Nut Muffins: Prepare as directed but substitute ¾ cup moderately finely chopped hickory nuts, pecans, walnuts, or black walnuts for dates. Makes about 1 dozen.

2¼ cups sifted
all-purpose flour

3 tablespoons granulated
sugar or raw sugar

1 tablespoon baking
powder

½ teaspoon salt

¾ cup finely diced pitted
dates (see Note
opposite)

1 cup milk

¼ cup vegetable oil or
melted unsalted butter

1 large egg, well beaten
with 1 teaspoon finely
grated orange or lemon
zest

1 Preheat oven to 400°F. Lightly grease 12 standard-size muffin pan cups or spritz with nonstick cooking spray or, if you prefer, insert a crinkly muffin liner into each cup. Set pans aside.

2 Combine flour, sugar, baking powder, and salt in medium mixing bowl, add dates, and toss well to mix. Make well in center of dry ingredients, and set aside.

3 Whisk milk with oil and egg mixture in small bowl until smooth, pour into well in dry ingredients, and stir only enough to combine—specks of flour should be clearly visible in batter.

4 Spoon batter into muffin pans, dividing amount equally— each muffin pan cup will be approximately two-thirds full, though occasionally a bit more or a bit less.

5 Slide onto middle oven shelf and bake 20 to 25 minutes until muffins have risen and their tops are nicely rounded and evenly browned.

6 Serve hot with plenty of unsalted butter.

Herb Garden Muffins

makes about
1 dozen

I've always grown my own herbs, things like bay leaves, chives, parsley, rosemary, sage, and thyme—especially lemon thyme. All the years I lived in New York, I turned my south-facing windowsills into herb gardens. Amazing what you can grow in eight-inch terracotta pots. It didn't take me long, however, to discover that certain herbs fared better because they were impervious to the aphids and white flies that zeroed in on the tender leaves of basil, parsley, and tarragon. So I'd concentrate on the herbs that thrived. When I moved south and had a big outdoor planter box, I discovered that the herbs that thrived on my Gramercy Park windowsills also thrived in the planter box. But the more delicate, alas, proved to be "deer candy." So I now grow only the deer-proof ones—things like bay leaves, rosemary, sage, and thyme. Fortunately, the tender-leafed herbs can be bought at the nearest farmer's market. Even local supermarkets now sell little plastic packets of fresh herbs. The recipe that follows should be made only with fresh herbs because they impart true herb fragrance and flavor. For that reason, I give no dried herb equivalents.

2 cups sifted all-purpose flour

¼ cup freshly grated Parmigiano-Reggiano

1 tablespoon baking powder

1 tablespoon granulated sugar or raw sugar

½ teaspoon salt

¼ teaspoon freshly ground black pepper

1 cup milk

¼ cup (½ stick) unsalted butter, melted

1 large egg

¼ cup moderately coarsely chopped fresh Italian (flat-leaf) parsley

2 tablespoons moderately finely snipped fresh chives

1 tablespoon moderately finely snipped fresh lemon thyme

1 Preheat oven to 400°F. Lightly grease 12 standard-size muffin pan cups or spritz with nonstick cooking spray or, if you prefer, insert a crinkly muffin liner into each cup. Set pans aside.

2 Combine first six ingredients (flour through black pepper) in medium mixing bowl, make well in center of dry ingredients, and set aside.

3 Whisk milk, butter, and egg in small bowl until frothy, then mix in parsley, chives, and thyme. Pour into well in dry ingredients, and stir only enough to combine—specks of flour should be visible in batter.

4 Spoon batter into muffin pans, dividing amount equally—each muffin pan cup will be approximately two-thirds full, though occasionally a bit more or a bit less.

5 Slide onto middle oven shelf and bake 20 to 25 minutes until muffins have risen and their tops are nicely rounded and evenly browned.

6 Serve hot with plenty of unsalted butter.

VARIATION:

Herb Garden Corn Muffins: Prepare as directed but substitute 1 cup yellow cornmeal (not stone-ground) for 1 cup sifted all-purpose flour. Makes about 1 dozen.

Parmesan-Crusted Muffins

makes about 1 dozen standard-size muffins or 10 muffin tops

Is there anyone who doesn't go for garlic bread? Or cheese bread? Not likely. So I worked up a recipe built around these two that could be baked either as muffins or as muffin tops for those who like the "crust" even more than the muffin. **Note:** *If the olive oil used in both the muffins and the topping is to absorb enough fresh garlic flavor, heat it briefly—I do it by microwave and allow the garlic to steep in the warm oil while I ready the other ingredients. I also prepare the topping first so it's ready to use the instant the muffin batter is in the pan.*

Garlic Oil (see Note above):

¼ cup plus 2 tablespoons extra-virgin olive oil

1 large garlic clove, smashed and skin removed

Topping:

¼ cup moderately fine soft white bread crumbs

2½ tablespoons freshly grated Parmigiano-Reggiano

1 tablespoon moderately finely chopped Italian (flat-leaf) parsley

½ teaspoon dried thyme leaves, crumbled

¼ teaspoon freshly ground black pepper

2 tablespoons Garlic Oil (see Note above)

Muffins:

2 cups sifted all-purpose flour

¼ cup freshly grated Parmigiano-Reggiano

2 teaspoons baking powder

½ teaspoon baking soda

½ teaspoon salt

½ teaspoon dried thyme leaves, crumbled

½ teaspoon freshly ground black pepper

1 cup buttermilk (not fat-free)

¼ cup Garlic Oil (see Note above)

1 large egg, lightly beaten

1 Preheat oven to 400°F. Lightly grease 12 standard-size muffin pan cups or spritz with nonstick cooking spray, or insert a crinkly muffin liner into each cup. Set pans aside. Or, if you prefer, spritz 10 muffin top pan cups with nonstick cooking spray.

2 **Garlic Oil:** Pour oil into 2-cup oven-proof glass measuring cup and drop in garlic. Microwave on Low (about 25 percent power) until oil quivers— 3 to 5 minutes. Remove from micro-wave and let steep briefly; before using, discard garlic.

3 **Topping:** Combine all ingredients except Garlic Oil in small bowl, then drizzle 2 tablespoons oil over all, toss well, and set aside.

4 **Muffins:** Whisk first seven ingredients (flour through black pepper) together in medium mixing bowl, make well in center of dry ingredients, and set aside.

5 Beat buttermilk, remaining $\frac{1}{4}$ cup Garlic Oil, and egg well in small bowl, pour into well in dry ingredients, and stir only enough to combine—batter should be lumpy and specks of flour clearly visible.

6 Divide batter among 12 standard-size muffin pan cups—each cup will be approximately two-thirds full, though occasionally a bit more or a bit less. Or spoon batter into 10 muffin top pan cups, dividing amount equally and spreading to edge of each cup. Sprinkle topping evenly over each muffin or muffin top.

7 Slide onto middle oven shelf and bake full-size muffins about 20 minutes and muffin tops about 12 minutes, or until muffins have risen and topping is richly browned.

8 Serve at once—no butter needed. Anything else either.

Sour Cream 'n' Onion Muffins

makes about 1 dozen standard-size muffins or about 2½ dozen mini muffins

I'm forever improvising, dreaming up new recipes. For this one, I wanted to capture the intense onion flavor and can't-get-enough-of-it-ness of California Dip, that cocktail party favorite that's nothing more than a packet of dried onion soup mix folded into sour cream. Took a bit of trial and error, I'll admit, but I think the results justify it. **Note:** *If you'd like to serve these warm as party snacks, bake in mini muffin pans for 10 to 12 minutes. Serve with a little warmer of melted unsalted butter for dipping or with soft cream cheese that can be spread onto the muffins once they've been split. My good New York friend and colleague Joanne Hayes, who tried these muffins, remarked, "I think they would be great with barbecue, grilled steaks, or chicken. Also as part of a basket of mixed rolls."*

1 (1-ounce) packet dry onion soup mix

½ cup boiling water

2 cups sifted all-purpose flour

2 teaspoons baking powder

1 teaspoon sugar

½ teaspoon baking soda

1 (8-ounce) carton (1 cup) sour cream (not low-fat or fat-free)

1 large egg, beaten until frothy

1 Preheat oven to 400°F. Lightly grease 12 standard-size muffin pan cups or 30 minis or spritz with nonstick cooking spray, or if you prefer, insert a crinkly muffin liner into each cup. Set pans aside.

2 Meanwhile, place onion soup mix in small bowl, gradually stir in boiling water, and let stand on counter 15 minutes.

3 Combine flour, baking powder, sugar, and baking soda in medium mixing bowl, make well in center, and set aside.

4 When onion soup mixture has rested 15 minutes, whisk in sour cream and egg. Pour into well in dry ingredients, and stir only enough to combine—specks of flour should be clearly visible in batter.

5 Spoon batter into muffin pans, dividing amount equally—each muffin pan cup will be approximately two-thirds full, though occasionally a bit more or a bit less.

6 Slide onto middle oven shelf and bake about 20 minutes until muffins have risen and their tops are nicely rounded and evenly browned. **Note:** Mini muffins should be done in 12 to 14 minutes.

7 Serve warm or at room temperature with melted butter or softened cream cheese.

New England Blueberry Muffins with Maple Syrup

makes about
1 dozen

This is a recipe I picked up more than 25 years ago while in Vermont on assignment for *Family Circle* magazine. The beauty of it is that you can make it with fresh blueberries, frozen, even dried (½ cup is about right for this recipe). **Note:** *Use only pure maple syrup for this recipe and here's a secret: Grade B has richer, deeper flavor than Grade A and can be ordered online, as can granulated maple sugar (see Sources, page 220).*

2 cups sifted all-purpose flour

2 tablespoons granulated maple or raw sugar

1 tablespoon baking powder

½ teaspoon salt

⅞ cup milk

¼ cup (½ stick) unsalted butter, melted, or ¼ cup vegetable oil

1 large egg, beaten with 2 tablespoons pure maple syrup (see Note above) and ¼ teaspoon finely grated orange or lemon zest

1 cup fresh blueberries, stemmed, washed, and patted dry on paper toweling, or 1 package (10 ounces) frozen blueberries, thawed, drained, and patted dry (see headnote)

1 Preheat oven to 400°F. Lightly grease 12 standard-size muffin pan cups or spritz with nonstick cooking spray or, if you prefer, insert a crinkly muffin liner into each cup. Set pans aside.

2 Combine flour, sugar, baking powder, and salt in medium mixing bowl. Make well in center of dry ingredients, and set aside.

3 Whisk milk, butter, and egg mixture in small bowl until smooth, pour into well in dry ingredients, and stir only enough to dampen. Fold blueberries in with the lightest of touches—flecks of flour should be visible in batter.

4 Spoon batter into muffin pans, dividing amount equally—each muffin pan cup will be approximately two-thirds full, though occasionally a bit more or a bit less.

5 Slide onto middle oven shelf and bake 20 to 25 minutes until muffins have risen and their tops are nicely rounded and evenly browned.

6 Serve at once with unsalted butter and, if you like, drizzles of pure maple syrup.

Bacon 'n' Eggs Breakfast Muffins

makes about 1 dozen

These are the muffins to make if you should have a leftover hard-cooked egg in the fridge and a few slices of crisp bacon. If not, you can get a jump on things by browning the bacon and hard-cooking the egg in advance. **Note:** *The best way to hard-cook an egg? See page 22. Once the egg's cooked and shelled, pop it into a small plastic zipper bag and refrigerate until ready to use.*

2 cups sifted all-purpose flour

1 tablespoon baking powder

1 teaspoon sugar

½ teaspoon salt

1 large hard-cooked egg, shelled and coarsely chopped (see Note above)

⅓ cup coarsely crumbled crisply cooked bacon (about 4 strips)

1 cup milk

1 large egg

3 tablespoons melted bacon drippings or unsalted butter

1 Preheat oven to 400°F. Lightly grease 12 standard-size muffin pan cups or spritz with nonstick cooking spray or, if you prefer, insert a crinkly muffin liner into each cup. Set pans aside.

2 Combine flour, baking powder, sugar, and salt in medium mixing bowl. Add hard-cooked egg and bacon, toss lightly to mix, make well in center of dry ingredients, and set aside.

3 Whisk milk with egg and bacon drippings in small bowl until frothy, pour into well in dry ingredients, and stir only enough to combine—specks of flour should be visible in batter.

4 Spoon batter into muffin pans, dividing amount equally— each muffin pan cup will be approximately two-thirds full, though occasionally a bit more or a bit less.

5 Slide onto middle oven shelf and bake about 20 minutes until muffins have risen and their tops are nicely rounded and evenly browned.

6 Serve hot with plenty of unsalted butter.

Orange Muffins

makes about
1 dozen

For me, this is the quintessential breakfast muffin—delicious with ham and eggs, delicious with bacon and eggs, perfect even with a cup of coffee on the run or glass of freshly squeezed orange juice. Note *freshly squeezed*—that's key.

2¼ cups sifted all-purpose flour

¼ cup raw sugar or light brown sugar (do not pack)

2½ teaspoons baking powder

½ teaspoon baking soda

¼ teaspoon salt

¼ teaspoon freshly grated nutmeg

½ cup milk or evaporated milk (my choice because of its slightly caramel flavor; not low-fat or fat-free)

¼ cup (½ stick) unsalted butter, melted

1 large egg, well beaten

1 tablespoon finely grated orange zest

1 teaspoon finely grated lemon zest

½ cup freshly squeezed orange juice

1 Preheat oven to 400°F. Lightly grease 12 standard-size muffin pan cups or spritz with nonstick cooking spray or, if you prefer, insert a crinkly muffin liner into each cup. Set pans aside.

2 Combine first six ingredients (flour through nutmeg) in medium mixing bowl, make well in center of dry ingredients, and set aside.

3 Whisk milk with butter, egg, and orange and lemon zests in small bowl until frothy. Add orange juice, and beat until smooth. Pour into well in dry ingredients, and stir only enough to combine—specks of flour should be clearly visible in batter.

4 Spoon batter into muffin pans, dividing amount equally—each muffin pan cup will be approximately two-thirds full, though occasionally a bit more or a bit less.

5 Slide onto middle oven shelf and bake 20 to 25 minutes until muffins have risen and their tops are nicely rounded and evenly browned.

6 Serve hot with plenty of unsalted butter. I also like to put out orange or ginger marmalade, sometimes in place of butter, sometimes in addition to it.

VARIATIONS:

Orange-Almond Muffins: Prepare as directed but add ½ to ⅔ cup moderately finely chopped toasted slivered almonds (about 5 to 8 minutes in a 350°F oven, then cooled) to combined dry ingredients and toss well. Make well in center of dry ingredients, then follow steps 3 through 6. Makes about 1 dozen.

Orange-Pecan Muffins: Prepare as directed but add ½ to ⅔ cup moderately finely chopped pecans to combined dry ingredients and toss well. Make well in center of dry ingredients, then follow steps 3 through 6. Makes about 1 dozen.

Orange-Cranberry Muffins: Prepare as directed but add ½ to ⅔ cup moderately finely chopped dried cranberries to combined dry ingredients and toss well. Make well in center of dry ingredients, then follow steps 3 through 6. Makes about 1 dozen.

Orange-Blueberry Muffins: Prepare as directed but add ½ to ⅔ cup moderately finely chopped dried blueberries to combined dry ingredients and toss well. Make well in center of dry ingredients, then follow steps 3 through 6. Makes about 1 dozen.

Toasted Benne Seed Muffins

makes about 1 dozen

Benne are what folks in Charleston and the South Carolina Lowcountry call sesame seeds. They were brought to the Lowcountry by African slaves, who considered them good luck and planted them around their cabins. Soon good plantation cooks were stirring them into biscuits, cookies, and candies and they remain Lowcountry favorites to this day. So, I thought, why not benne muffins? **Note:** *For directions on how to toast sesame seeds, see Benne (Sesame) Seeds, page 17.*

2 cups sifted all-purpose flour

1 tablespoon raw sugar

2 ½ teaspoons baking powder

¼ teaspoon baking soda

½ teaspoon salt

¼ cup lightly toasted sesame seeds (see Note above)

1 cup buttermilk (not fat-free)

1 large egg

3 tablespoons vegetable oil blended with 1 teaspoon Asian toasted sesame oil

1 Preheat oven to 400°F. Lightly grease 12 standard-size muffin pan cups or spritz with nonstick cooking spray or, if you prefer, insert a crinkly muffin liner into each cup. Set pans aside.

2 Combine first five ingredients (flour through salt) in medium mixing bowl. Set 1 tablespoon sesame seeds aside; add remaining sesame seeds to flour mixture, toss well, make well in center of dry ingredients, and set aside.

3 Beat buttermilk, egg, and oil mixture in small bowl until smooth. Pour into well in dry ingredients and stir only enough to combine—you should see specks of flour in the batter.

4 Spoon batter into muffin pans, dividing amount equally—each muffin pan cup will be approximately two-thirds full, though occasionally a bit more or a bit less. Sprinkle reserved sesame seeds on top of unbaked muffins, again dividing amount evenly.

5 Slide onto middle oven shelf and bake about 20 minutes until muffins have risen and their tops are gently rounded and lightly browned.

6 Serve at once with plenty of unsalted butter. Or cool to room temperature before serving.

VARIATION:

Benne Corn Muffins: Prepare as directed substituting 1 cup yellow cornmeal (not stone-ground) for 1 cup all-purpose flour. Makes about 1 dozen.

VARIATION:

Smoky Country Ham and Cheese Corn Muffins: Prepare as directed substituting 1 cup yellow cornmeal (not stone-ground) for 1 cup all-purpose flour. Makes about 1 dozen.

Smoky Country Ham and Cheese Muffins

makes about 1 dozen

Although a pink packing-house ham can be used in this recipe, a good country ham (Virginia, Kentucky, etc.) is vastly superior (see Sources, page 220). But whatever ham you use must be fully cooked, ready-to-eat because muffins bake so fast. The cheese to use? Smoked Gouda, which nearly every supermarket sells. **Note:** *Because of the saltiness of the ham and cheese, there's no additional salt in this recipe.*

2 cups sifted all-purpose flour

1 tablespoon sugar

2 teaspoons baking powder

1 teaspoon baking soda

½ cup moderately coarsely shredded smoked Gouda cheese

⅓ cup moderately finely chopped fully cooked country ham (see headnote)

1 cup buttermilk (not fat-free)

1 large egg

¼ cup (½ stick) unsalted butter, melted

1 Preheat oven to 400°F. Lightly grease 12 standard-size muffin pan cups or spritz with nonstick cooking spray or, if you prefer, insert a crinkly muffin liner into each cup. Set pans aside.

2 Combine flour, sugar, baking powder, and baking soda in medium mixing bowl. Add cheese and ham, toss well, make well in center of dry ingredients, and set aside.

3 Beat buttermilk, egg, and butter in small bowl until smooth. Pour into well in dry ingredients and stir only enough to combine—specks of flour should be visible.

4 Spoon batter into muffin pans, dividing amount equally—each muffin pan cup will be approximately two-thirds full, though occasionally a bit more or a bit less in batter.

5 Slide onto middle oven shelf and bake 20 to 25 minutes until muffins have risen and their tops are gently rounded and lightly browned.

6 Serve at once with plenty of unsalted butter. Or cool to room temperature before serving.

Pepperoni Muffins with Sun-Dried Tomatoes

makes about 1 dozen

Turns out our favorite pizza topping is not Italian. According to John Mariani (*How Italian Food Conquered the World*), pepperoni is "purely an Italian-American creation." But that makes it no less delicious—on pizza or stirred into muffins along with sun-dried tomatoes. **Note:** *For ¼ cup finely diced rehydrated sun-dried tomatoes, you'll need about six halves. To rehydrate, soak 15 minutes in just enough very hot water to cover, then drain well and pat dry on paper toweling.*

2 cups sifted all-purpose flour

¼ cup freshly grated Parmigiano-Reggiano

1 tablespoon baking powder

1 tablespoon raw sugar

¼ teaspoon salt

½ cup moderately finely diced pepperoni

¼ cup moderately finely diced rehydrated sun-dried tomatoes (see Note above)

1 cup milk

3 tablespoons extra-virgin olive oil or melted unsalted butter

1 large egg

1 Preheat oven to 400°F. Lightly grease 12 standard-size muffin pan cups or spritz with nonstick cooking spray or, if you prefer, insert a crinkly muffin liner into each cup. Set pans aside.

2 Combine first five ingredients (flour through salt) in medium mixing bowl. Add pepperoni and tomatoes, toss well, make well in center of dry ingredients, and set aside.

3 Whisk milk, oil, and egg in small bowl until frothy. Pour into well in dry ingredients and stir only enough to combine—specks of flour should be visible in batter.

4 Spoon batter into muffin pans, dividing amount equally—each muffin pan cup will be approximately two-thirds full, though occasionally a bit more or a bit less.

5 Slide onto middle oven shelf and bake 20 to 25 minutes until muffins have risen and their tops are nicely rounded and evenly browned.

6 Serve oven-hot with plenty of unsalted butter.

Pimiento Cheese Muffins

makes about 1 dozen

Southern novelist Reynolds Price once described pimiento cheese as "the peanut butter of my childhood." My own childhood memories? I remember vats of freshly made pimiento cheese at small groceries now long gone; I remember little jars of it mass-produced for Southern consumption; I even remember making it myself. Now, decades later, I've folded pimiento cheese into a fairly classic muffin recipe and then sometimes "butter" the split muffins with more pimiento cheese (see page 206).

2 cups sifted all-purpose flour

2 teaspoons baking powder

½ teaspoon baking soda

½ teaspoon salt

1 cup buttermilk (not fat-free) blended with ⅓ cup firmly packed pimiento cheese (see headnote)

1 large egg

¼ cup vegetable oil or melted unsalted butter

1 Preheat oven to 400°F. Lightly grease 12 standard-size muffin pan cups or spritz with nonstick cooking spray or, if you prefer, insert a crinkly muffin liner into each cup. Set pans aside.

2 Combine flour, baking powder, soda, and salt in medium mixing bowl, make well in center of dry ingredients, and set aside.

3 Whisk buttermilk mixture with egg and oil in small bowl until frothy. Pour into well in dry ingredients and stir only enough to combine—specks of flour should be visible in batter.

4 Spoon batter into muffin pans, dividing amount equally—each muffin pan cup will be approximately two-thirds full, though occasionally a bit more or a bit less.

5 Slide onto middle oven shelf and bake 20 to 25 minutes until muffins have risen and their tops are nicely rounded and evenly browned.

6 Serve hot with plenty of unsalted butter.

Falafel Muffin Tops

makes about
1 dozen

While spending time in Lebanon, Israel, and Jordan, I developed a taste for falafel, those chickpea fritters served in or out of pita bread with slatherings of hummus. Then when I came home to New York, I could indulge my passion by strolling two blocks up Lexington Avenue to Twenty-third Street and a fast-food place that specialized in falafel. Sadly, I've yet to find good falafel in Piedmont, North Carolina, where I now live, but I have noticed boxes of falafel mix at one of my supermarkets and that got me to thinking. Could I work up a muffin recipe with baked-in falafel flavors? Indeed, but these, mind you, are thinner muffin tops, not plump standard-size muffins. I break them open while hot (or still warm) and spread with the hummus that nearly every supermarket now sells—not only the classic version but also spin-offs with more garlic or sweet red pepper paste or sun-dried tomatoes blended in. I also like to make my own hummus (see recipe, page 210).

1 cup sifted all-purpose flour

¾ cup falafel mix (1 envelope from a 2-envelope, 6.3-ounce package; see headnote)

2 teaspoons baking powder

1 teaspoon ground coriander

½ teaspoon baking soda

½ teaspoon freshly ground black pepper

¼ teaspoon salt

1 cup buttermilk (not fat-free)

¼ cup firmly packed hummus (see headnote)

2 tablespoons vegetable oil

1 large egg, well beaten with 1 teaspoon Asian toasted sesame oil and 1 large garlic clove that has been crushed in a garlic press

2 tablespoons coarsely chopped fresh cilantro

2 tablespoons coarsely chopped Italian (flat-leaf) parsley

1 Preheat oven to 425°F. Spritz each of 12 standard size muffin top pan cups with nonstick cooking spray, and set aside.

2 Combine first seven ingredients (flour through salt) in medium mixing bowl, make well in center of dry ingredients, and set aside.

3 Whisk buttermilk, hummus, oil, and egg mixture in small bowl until smooth, then mix in cilantro and parsley. Pour into well in dry ingredients, and stir only enough to combine—floury specks should show in batter.

4 Spoon batter into muffin top pan cups, dividing amount equally and spreading evenly.

5 Slide onto middle oven shelf and bake 12 to 15 minutes until puffed and golden brown.

6 Serve hot or warm with plenty of hummus. I even like these at room temperature.

PB & J Muffins

makes about
1 dozen

Is there a kid—big or little—who doesn't adore PB & J sandwiches? So why not PB & J muffins? They're almost as fast as sandwiches and in my opinion, even better.

2 cups sifted all-purpose flour

1 tablespoon baking powder

2 tablespoons raw sugar (optional)

½ teaspoon salt

1¼ cups evaporated milk (not low-fat or fat-free)

⅔ cup firmly packed chunky peanut butter

1 large egg

2 tablespoons peanut oil or melted unsalted butter

¼ cup grape jelly

1 Preheat oven to 400°F. Lightly grease 12 standard-size muffin pan cups or spritz with nonstick cooking spray or, if you prefer, insert a crinkly muffin liner into each cup. Set pans aside.

2 Combine flour, baking powder, sugar (if using), and salt in medium mixing bowl, make well in center of dry ingredients, and set aside.

3 Whisk milk, peanut butter, egg, and oil in small bowl until well blended. Pour into well in dry ingredients and stir only enough to combine—flecks of flour should be visible in batter.

4 Spoon batter into muffin pans, dividing amount equally—each muffin pan cup will be approximately two-thirds full, though occasionally a bit more or a bit less.

5 Slide onto middle oven shelf and bake 20 to 25 minutes until muffins have risen and their tops are nicely rounded and evenly browned.

6 Using a sharp paring knife, cut a small divot out of the top of each still-warm muffin, spoon in 1 level teaspoon jelly, then replace divot.

7 Serve warm or at room temperature. No butter needed.

Zucchini Muffins

makes about
1 dozen standard-size
muffins or
8 muffin tops

Most zucchini muffins are as sweet as cupcakes, but not these, which contain freshly grated Parmigiano-Reggiano, fresh herbs, and just enough raw sugar to mellow things. Serve them at breakfast, lunch, or dinner. Or enjoy as a between-meals snack. And by all means, try the Curried Zucchini Muffins, which follow.

2 cups sifted all-purpose flour

¼ cup freshly grated Parmigiano-Reggiano

2 tablespoons raw sugar

1 tablespoon baking powder

¼ teaspoon salt

¼ teaspoon freshly ground black pepper

1 cup milk

3 tablespoons extra-virgin olive oil

1 large egg

1 cup coarsely shredded zucchini (about 1 medium)

2 tablespoons coarsely chopped Italian (flat-leaf) parsley

1 tablespoon finely chopped fresh oregano or marjoram or 1 teaspoon dried oregano or marjoram leaves, crumbled

1 teaspoon finely chopped fresh thyme or ¼ teaspoon dried thyme leaves, crumbled

1 Preheat oven to 400°F. Lightly grease 12 standard-size muffin pan cups or spritz with nonstick cooking spray, or insert a crinkly muffin liner into each cup. Set pans aside. Or, if you prefer, spritz 8 muffin top pan cups with nonstick cooking spray.

2 Combine first six ingredients (flour through black pepper) in medium-size mixing bowl, make well in center of dry ingredients, and set aside.

3 Whisk milk, oil, and egg in second medium bowl until frothy, then mix in all remaining ingredients. Pour into well in dry ingredients, and stir only enough to combine—specks of flour should be visible in batter.

4 Divide batter among 12 standard-size muffin pan cups—each cup will be approximately two-thirds full, though occasionally a bit more or a bit less. Or spoon batter into 8 muffin top pan cups, dividing amount equally and spreading to edge of each cup.

5 Slide onto middle oven shelf. Bake full-size muffins 20 to 25 minutes and muffin tops 12 to 14 minutes or until muffins or muffin tops have risen and are nicely browned.

6 Serve oven-hot with plenty of unsalted butter or, if you prefer, little dipping bowls of extra-virgin olive oil.

Curried Zucchini Muffins

makes about
1 dozen

Until I went to India, I was unaware of the number of vegetables curried there—everything from cabbage to cauliflower to green peas to potatoes to eggplants called "brinjals." I'm so fond of curry I've been currying all of these vegetables and coarsely grated zucchini as well ever since. Then it occurred to me: Why not see if curried zucchini could be folded into a basic muffin batter? If you like curry, I think you'll like the results. **Note:** *Ghee is nothing more than melted unsalted butter from which the milk solids have been skimmed—pure gold.* **Tip:** *To save time, sauté the zucchini and scallions in advance and refrigerate until 15 to 20 minutes before using—use that time to bring the mixture to room temperature.*

¼ cup ghee (see Note above)

1 cup coarsely shredded young zucchini (2 to 3 small)

2 medium scallions, trimmed and coarsely chopped (include some green tops)

1 tablespoon curry powder

2 cups sifted all-purpose flour

1 tablespoon baking powder

½ teaspoon salt

⅛ teaspoon ground hot red pepper (cayenne), or to taste

1 (5-ounce) can evaporated milk (not low-fat or fat-free)

⅓ cup chicken or vegetable broth

1 large egg beaten with 2 table-spoons finely chopped mango chutney

1 Preheat oven to 400°F. Lightly grease 12 standard-size muffin pan cups or spritz with nonstick cooking spray or, if you prefer, insert a crinkly muffin liner into each cup. Set pans aside.

2 Heat ghee in small heavy skillet over moderate heat until ripples appear on pan bottom—about 1 minute. Add zucchini and scallions and sauté, stirring often, just until limp and golden—2 to 3 minutes. Blend in curry powder and heat, stirring constantly, about 1 minute more to temper the raw curry taste. Remove from heat and reserve.

3 Whisk flour with baking powder, salt, and cayenne in medium mixing bowl, make well in center of dry ingredients, and set aside.

4 In second medium bowl, beat milk, broth, and egg mixture until well blended, then stir in reserved zucchini mixture. Pour into well in dry ingredients and stir only enough to mix—specks of flour should be clearly visible.

5 Spoon batter into muffin pans, dividing amount equally—each muffin pan cup will be approximately two-thirds full, though occasionally a bit more or a bit less.

6 Slide onto middle oven shelf and bake 20 to 25 minutes until muffins have risen and their tops are gently rounded and lightly browned.

7 Serve at once with a little bowl of warm ghee and/or sieved mango chutney. I also like these muffins with good old-fashioned apple butter, apple jelly, or orange or ginger marmalade—no ghee needed.

English Muffins

According to Alan Davidson (*The Oxford Companion to Food*), English muffins were "usually cooked on a griddle, which gives a flat, golden brown top and bottom . . . and a spongy interior." He adds that the recipe first appeared in print in England in Hannah Glasse's *The Art of Cookery Made Plain and Easy* (1747) under the heading "To make Muffings and Oat-Cakes." Her directions are wordy and measurements vague but her instructions for eating hot-off-the-griddle muffins are spot-on: ". . . don't touch them with a Knife, either to spread or cut them open, if you do they will be as heavy as Lead. . . ."

Further research shows that even today English muffins are often cooked the eighteenth-century way—on a griddle. And that got me to thinking. Couldn't they be baked in an oven? In a single batch instead of two or three on the stove top? Absolutely.

2 cups sifted unbleached
   all-purpose flour

1¼ cups sifted bread flour (about)

1¼ teaspoons salt

½ cup very warm water (105° to
   115°F)

1 (¼-ounce) package active dry
   yeast

1½ teaspoons sugar

¾ cup milk, scalded and cooled
   to between 105° and 115°F

1 tablespoon cornmeal (not
   stone-ground)

1 Sift two flours and salt onto piece of wax paper, empty into sturdy electric mixer bowl fitted with mixing paddle, and set aside.

2 Place warm water in small bowl, add yeast and sugar, stir until dissolved, then let stand uncovered until frothy—about 5 minutes.

3 Pour yeast mixture into mixer bowl, add warm milk, and beat until stiff dough forms, adding a bit more bread flour, if needed, or a little more hot water. Remove mixing paddle, insert dough hook, and knead dough until supple and elastic—about 1 minute.

4 Turn dough into large buttered or oiled bowl, and turn buttered side up. Cover with wax paper, set in warm spot, and let rise until doubled in bulk—about 30 minutes.

5 Punch dough down, turn onto lightly floured surface, and knead gently—about 1 minute. Shape into ball, return to buttered bowl, turn buttered side up, and cover with wax paper. Set in warm spot and let rise 30 minutes.

6 Meanwhile, lightly oil 8 muffin top pan cups or spritz with nonstick cooking spray, and set aside. Also sprinkle large sheet of wax paper with cornmeal, distributing evenly, and set aside.

7 Punch dough down and knead gently until smooth. Divide dough into 8 balls of equal size, then shape into 8 burger-like patties about 3 inches across. Arrange, not touching, on cornmeal-sprinkled wax paper, then turn so both sides of each patty are lightly coated with cornmeal.

8 Set patties in muffin top pan cups, cover with wax paper, and let rise 30 minutes. After 10 minutes, preheat oven to 400°F.

9 Slide muffins onto middle oven shelf and bake 5 minutes, reduce oven temperature to 350°F and bake 15 minutes longer or until lightly browned.

10 Serve oven-hot with plenty of unsalted butter.

Corn
MUFFINS
Plain
& Fancy

Growing up in the small-town South, I soon discovered that my mother was the only woman in our neighborhood who made muffins. She was different, a Yankee from the state of Illinois, whose corn muffins were "to die for."

Our neighbors, thoroughly Southern, indeed North Carolina born-and-bred, ate fresh-baked biscuits three times a day. To be honest, I don't remember eating muffins in my hometown until I was quite grown up. Except in my own house.

Then when I was in my early twenties, I remember lunching at a local tearoom and there in the bread basket, bundled in a crisp white linen napkin, were corn muffins right out of the oven. But not the kind my mother made with granular yellow meal. These were white inside, feathery as cake, because they'd been made with stone-ground meal.

Back then Crabtree Creek on the north side of Raleigh kept Lassiter Mill's creaky wooden wheel grinding out the floury cornmeal Southerners insisted upon—usually white but sometimes yellow. The corn it ground wasn't sweet corn,

which my Midwestern family adored, but a less sweet variety called "field corn." But when dried, then ground, its meal was deliciously nutty. Though Lassiter Mill is just a memory, there is no shortage of old-timey water-driven mills below the Mason-Dixon (see Sources, page 220).

Southern supermarkets sell a variety of stone-ground meals; in fact, the big-brand granular yellow meal my mother used is increasingly difficult to find down South, although it's ubiquitous everywhere else.

In the pages that follow, you'll find muffins made with both types of cornmeal: Old-Timey Down South Corn Muffins . . . Corn Muffins with Cracklin's . . . All-American Corn Muffins . . . Corn Muffins with Country Sausage . . . Curried Sweet Potato Corn Muffins.

And these are just a sampling.

Old-Timey Down South Corn Muffins

makes about
1 dozen

I was quite grown up before I tasted honest-to-God Southern muffins made with stone-ground cornmeal even though I'd grown up in Raleigh, North Carolina. All the years my Illinois mother lived down South, she clung to the recipes of her youth (see All-American Corn Muffins, which follows). So it was only when I went to work as an assistant home demonstration agent in Iredell County, North Carolina, that I learned how to make muffins with stone-ground cornmeal. Sorry, Mother, but they're now my favorite. Of course, the fastest way to start an argument down South is to mention the word "sugar." Southerners are of two minds about it: traditionalists who insist that no proper corn bread contains even a grain of sugar and other Southerners who slip in a tablespoon or two to heighten the corn flavor. Me? I sometimes add a tad of sugar, sometimes not. I think it depends on the recipe and, of course, on personal taste and conviction. Then there's the matter of the cornmeal itself. White or yellow? The old-time Southerners I know all insist upon white stone-ground cornmeal because it's traditional. I do, however, think the yellow has a bit more flavor and, of course, color. My advice? Suit yourself. **Note:** *If you use bacon drippings in this recipe, no need for additional salt, but if you use lard or corn oil, add ½ teaspoon salt.*

1¼ cups unsifted stone-
    ground cornmeal
    (white or yellow)

¾ cup sifted all-purpose
    flour

1 tablespoon baking
    powder

1 tablespoon sugar

½ teaspoon salt (optional;
    see Note opposite)

¼ teaspoon freshly
    ground black pepper

1 cup milk

¼ cup melted bacon
    drippings or lard (not
    vegetable shortening)
    or ¼ cup corn or other
    vegetable oil (see Note
    opposite)

1 large egg

1 Preheat oven to 400°F. Lightly grease 12 standard-size muffin pan cups or spritz with nonstick cooking spray or, if you prefer, insert a crinkly muffin liner into each cup. Set pans aside.

2 Combine first six ingredients (cornmeal through black pepper) in medium mixing bowl. Make well in center of dry ingredients, and set aside.

3 Whisk milk and bacon drippings with egg in small bowl until frothy, pour into well in dry ingredients, and stir only enough to combine—batter should be lumpy.

4 Spoon batter into muffin pans, dividing amount equally—each muffin pan cup will be approximately two-thirds full, though occasionally a bit more or a bit less.

5 Slide onto shelf in lower third of oven and bake 20 to 25 minutes until muffins have risen and their tops are nicely rounded and lightly browned.

6 Serve at once with plenty of unsalted butter.

All-American Corn Muffins

makes about 1 dozen

My mother's corn muffins—like her mother's—depended upon the granular yellow cornmeal every supermarket sold. And in my own travels about this country—beyond the South, that is—Mother's muffins seem to be everyone's "old reliable." But do try the variation that follows, which contains a new-to-me product—freeze-dried corn powder. Substituting it for some of the flour in this more or less classic corn muffin recipe injects dried corn flavor—you'll notice the aroma as the muffins bake. Finer textured than your everyday corn muffin, these are best served hot with plenty of unsalted butter. So where can you buy freeze-dried corn powder? See Sources (page 220).

1 cup sifted all-purpose flour

1 cup yellow cornmeal (not stone-ground)

2 tablespoons sugar

1 tablespoon baking powder

½ teaspoon salt

¼ teaspoon freshly ground black pepper (optional)

1 cup milk

¼ cup corn or other vegetable oil

1 large egg

1 Preheat oven to 400°F. Lightly grease 12 standard-size muffin pan cups or spritz with nonstick cooking spray or, if you prefer, insert a crinkly muffin liner into each cup. Set pans aside.

2 Combine first six ingredients (flour through black pepper, if using) in medium mixing bowl. Make well in center of dry ingredients and set aside.

3 Whisk milk and oil with egg in small bowl until frothy, pour into well in dry ingredients, and stir only enough to combine—batter should be lumpy.

4 Spoon batter into muffin pans, dividing amount equally—each muffin pan cup will be approximately two-thirds full, though occasionally a bit more or a bit less.

5 Slide onto middle oven shelf and bake about 20 minutes until muffins have risen and their tops are nicely rounded and evenly browned.

6 Serve at once with plenty of unsalted butter.

VARIATION:

Full-of-Flavor Corn Muffins: Reduce all-purpose flour to $^3/_4$ cup, add $^1/_4$ cup unsifted freeze-dried corn powder (see head-note) and 2 tablespoons freshly grated Parmigiano-Reggiano. Also substitute 2 tablespoons raw sugar or light brown sugar (do not pack) for granulated sugar. Once these changes are made, proceed as recipe directs. Makes about 1 dozen.

Corn Muffins with Cracklin's

Cracklin's, the crispy bits left over after pork fat has been rendered into lard, are prized by frugal Southern cooks who stir them into corn breads for added flavor. Above and beyond the Mason-Dixon, you're not likely to find pork fat for sale. But there's an easy solution. Ring the bell for the butcher and he'll probably be happy to give you some. Just make sure the skin's been removed. Cracklin's aren't difficult to make but they do take time, so you may want to prepare them ahead of time and store in the refrigerator or freezer until you're ready to make the muffins (no need to thaw frozen cracklin's before using). **Note:** *Many Southern cooks also save the cracklin' drippings. Store drippings in the refrigerator in a small tightly capped preserving jar, then use just as you would bacon drippings. That is, to season collards, turnip salad (greens), black-eyed peas, and such as well as to shorten biscuits, muffins, and other quick breads. Adds "meaty flavor," they say, though it's usually best to substitute the drippings for no more than half the fat called for in a recipe.*

Cracklin's:

2 cups skinless pork fat, cut in ¼-inch dice (about 12 ounces)

1 cup boiling water

Muffins:

1½ cups unsifted stone-ground cornmeal (preferably white)

¾ cup sifted all-purpose flour

2 teaspoons baking powder

½ teaspoon baking soda

½ teaspoon salt

¼ teaspoon freshly ground black pepper

¾ cup cracklin's

1 cup buttermilk (not fat-free)

2 tablespoons melted cracklin' or bacon drippings mixed with 2 tablespoons corn oil or ¼ cup corn oil (see headnote)

1 large egg, well beaten

1 Cracklin's: Preheat oven to 300°F. Spread pork fat in small heavy non-reactive Dutch oven or deep skillet, add boiling water, stir well, cover, then slide onto lowest oven shelf and bake for 1 hour. Remove lid, stir well, then bake uncovered about 2½ hours longer, stirring every ½ hour or so until all fat has rendered out and only crisp brown bits remain in drippings.

2 Using small fine sieve, lift cracklin's to several thicknesses of paper toweling to drain. If not using right away, spoon into small airtight container or plastic zipper bag, seal, and store in freezer or refrigerator. Also, if you like, save drippings; simply strain into small preserving jar, cap, and store in refrigerator.

3 Muffins: Preheat oven to 400°F. Lightly grease 12 standard-size muffin pan cups, spritz with nonstick cooking spray, or if you prefer, insert a crinkly muffin liner into each cup. Set pans aside.

4 Combine first six ingredients (corn-meal through black pepper) in medium mixing bowl. Add cracklin's and toss well. Make well in center of dry ingredients and set aside.

5 Whisk buttermilk, drippings mixture, and egg in small bowl until smooth. Pour into well in dry ingredients and stir only enough to combine—specks of cornmeal and flour should be visible in batter.

6 Spoon batter into muffin pans, dividing amount equally—each muffin pan cup will be approximately two-thirds full, though occasionally a bit more or a bit less.

7 Slide onto middle oven shelf and bake 20 to 25 minutes until muffins have risen and their tops are nicely rounded and evenly browned.

8 Serve at once. Southerners would break the muffins open and spread with gobs of unsalted butter. Non-Southerners may prefer to drizzle them with honey.

Corn Gems

Containing both cornmeal and cream-style corn, these muffins are almost as moist as corn pudding. Split them while hot and, if you must, tuck in a lump of unsalted butter. I for one like them straight up. Incidental intelligence: Back in the 1940s and '50s, mini muffins were called "gems." Today that name seems to apply to muffins that are special or unique in some way. **Note:** *If you've mastered your food processor and have a quick trigger finger, you can mix these muffins by processor once you've creamed the corn. Add the sour cream, corn oil, and eggs to the creamed corn and pulse 4 to 5 times. Now add the combined dry ingredients and pulse 4 times—no more. It's critical not to overprocess the batter, so make sure that specks of flour are clearly visible. Further pulsing will toughen your muffins and that you surely don't want.*

2 cups frozen whole-kernel corn, thawed but not drained

2 medium scallions, trimmed and cut in ½-inch chunks (white parts only)

1 cup unsifted stone-ground yellow cornmeal

½ cup sifted all-purpose flour

1½ teaspoons baking powder

½ teaspoon baking soda

½ teaspoon salt

½ teaspoon dried thyme leaves, crumbled

½ teaspoon freshly ground black pepper

1 (8-ounce) carton (1 cup) sour cream (not low-fat or fat-free)

3 tablespoons corn oil mixed with 2 tablespoons melted bacon drippings or 5 tablespoons corn oil

2 large eggs, well beaten

1 Preheat oven to 375°F. Spritz 18 standard-size muffin pan cups or 36 minis with nonstick cooking spray and set aside.

2 Place thawed corn, corn liquid, and scallions in food processor and alternately pulse and churn until you have cream-style corn. Set aside.

3 Combine next seven ingredients (cornmeal through black pepper) in medium mixing bowl. Make well in center of dry ingredients and set aside.

4 Whisk sour cream, oil mixture, and eggs in second medium bowl until smooth, then fold in corn mixture. Scoop into well in dry ingredients and stir only enough to combine—specks of cornmeal and flour should be visible in batter.

5 Spoon batter into muffin pans, dividing amount equally—each muffin pan cup will be approximately two-thirds full, though occasionally a bit more or a bit less.

6 Slide onto middle oven shelf and bake 20 to 25 minutes for full-size muffins and 12 to 15 minutes for minis or until muffins have risen and their tops are nicely rounded and evenly browned.

7 Serve at once with or without unsalted butter.

Corn Muffins with Country Sausage

makes about 1 dozen

Southerners dote upon country sausage as much as they do corn muffins so I thought, why not combine the two in a single recipe? But where should the sausage go? Inside the muffins, on top, or on the bottom? Layering the sausage with the batter might mean soggy muffins, spooning it on top might mean overbrowned muffins. So I divided the browned, crumbled sausage among the empty muffin cups, then added the batter (made with granular cornmeal to keep the muffins from going soggy), and it worked just as I hoped it would—the batter held the sausage in place as the muffins baked, even as they were removed from their pans. **Note:** *You need bulk sausage meat for this recipe or, failing that, link sausages removed from their casings. Down South, one-pound packages of Neese's bulk sausage meat are widely available in three flavors—original, sage, and hot (any one of them a good choice here). To quote the website of this Greensboro, North Carolina, company: "We pride ourselves on being a family business that dates back nearly 100 years when J. T. Neese started selling sausage from a covered wagon. Today, the business is run by the fourth generation of Neeses with the fifth generation on the way." As for ordering sausage online, see Sources (page 220).*

½ pound bulk sausage meat (see Note, page 83)

1 cup sifted all-purpose flour

1 cup yellow cornmeal (not stone-ground)

1 tablespoon baking powder

½ teaspoon salt

½ teaspoon dried thyme leaves, crumbled

¼ teaspoon freshly ground black pepper

1 cup milk or evaporated milk (not low-fat or fat-free)

1 large egg

¼ cup vegetable oil or sausage drippings plus enough oil to total ¼ cup

1 Preheat oven to 400°F. Lightly grease 12 standard-size muffin pan cups or spritz with nonstick cooking spray. Set pans aside.

2 Crumble sausage meat into a medium skillet set over moderately high heat and cook, stirring often, until uniformly brown—about 10 minutes. Drain sausage on several thicknesses of paper toweling and set aside. Reserve drippings, if you like, and use in lieu of some of the vegetable oil.

3 Combine next six ingredients (flour through black pepper) in medium mixing bowl, make well in center of dry ingredients, and set aside.

4 Whisk milk with egg and oil in small bowl until frothy, pour into well in dry ingredients, and stir only enough to combine—there should be lumps in the batter and specks of flour clearly visible.

5 Spoon cooked sausage meat into muffin pan cups, dividing total amount evenly—approximately a rounded tablespoon per muffin pan cup. Spoon batter into muffin pans, again dividing amount equally—each muffin pan cup will be about two-thirds full, though occasionally a bit more or a bit less.

6 Slide onto middle oven shelf and bake 20 to 25 minutes until muffins have risen and their tops are nicely rounded and evenly browned.

7 Serve at once with or without unsalted butter.

Curried Sweet Potato Corn Muffins

makes about 1 dozen

I've always wondered why we insist on sugaring sweet potatoes, on combining them with canned crushed pineapple and topping them with marshmallows. In truth, sweet potatoes are not very sweet and that's the way I prefer them—baked in their skins, then their flesh pushed up and topped with pats of unsalted butter. For this recipe, I bake the potatoes but do not season them. Once tender, I score the top of each potato with an X, squeeze the flesh into a small bowl, and mash thoroughly with a potato masher. I've also buzzed the baked potatoes to a silky puree in the food processor. But then I have a bowl, blade, and lid to wash—not very efficient when I need only 1 cup mashed sweet potato.

1 cup sifted all-purpose flour

1 cup yellow cornmeal (not stone-ground)

2 tablespoons firmly packed light brown sugar

1 tablespoon curry powder

2 teaspoons baking powder

½ teaspoon baking soda

¼ teaspoon ground cumin

¼ teaspoon ground cinnamon

¼ teaspoon ground hot red pepper (cayenne)

1 cup firmly packed mashed unseasoned baked sweet potato (about 1 large)

1 cup buttermilk (not fat-free), blended with 2 tablespoons finely chopped mango chutney

¼ cup (½ stick) unsalted butter, melted

1 large egg, lightly beaten

1 Preheat oven to 400°F. Lightly grease 12 standard-size muffin pan cups or spritz with nonstick cooking spray or, if you prefer, insert a crinkly muffin liner into each cup. Set pans aside.

2 Whisk first nine ingredients (flour through cayenne) together in medium mixing bowl, make well in center of dry ingredients, and set aside.

3 Combine mashed sweet potato, buttermilk mixture, butter, and egg in second medium bowl, beating until smooth. Pour into well in dry ingredients, and stir only enough to combine—specks of flour should be clearly visible in batter.

4 Spoon batter into muffin pans, dividing amount equally—each muffin pan cup will be approximately two-thirds full, though occasionally a bit more or a bit less.

5 Slide onto middle oven shelf and bake 20 to 25 minutes until muffins have risen and their tops are nicely rounded and lightly browned.

6 Serve muffins at once with plenty of unsalted butter and/or a good mango chutney. I also like these spread with ginger or orange marmalade.

EASY ADD-ONS (TOSS WITH DRY INGREDIENTS BEFORE ADDING COMBINED LIQUIDS):

* ½ cup coarsely chopped pecans or walnuts

* ½ cup dark seedless raisins or dried currants

* ½ cup dried blueberries

* ½ cup coarsely chopped dried cranberries

Chili-Cheddar
Two-Corn Muffins

makes about
1 dozen

Chili and corn are such a good match I've teamed them here in muffins where variations are welcome. See the easy add-ons that follow, then dream up your own. You should have no trouble as long as you add no more than ½ cup of something crumbled, diced, or grated and, needless to add, as long as the flavors are compatible.

1 cup sifted all-purpose flour

1 cup yellow cornmeal (not stone-ground)

1 tablespoon baking powder

1 tablespoon raw sugar

2 teaspoons chili powder

½ teaspoon salt

½ teaspoon dried oregano leaves, crumbled (preferably Mexican oregano)

¼ teaspoon freshly ground black pepper

1 cup coarsely shredded sharp Cheddar cheese

1 cup milk or evaporated milk (not low-fat or fat-free)

1 large egg

3 tablespoons vegetable oil or melted bacon drippings

½ cup frozen whole-kernel corn, thawed, drained, and patted dry on paper toweling

1   Preheat oven to 400°F. Lightly grease 12 standard-size muffin pan cups or spritz with nonstick cooking spray or, if you prefer, insert a crinkly muffin liner into each cup. Set pans aside.

2   Combine first eight ingredients (flour through black pepper) in medium mixing bowl. Add cheese and toss well to mix. Make well in center of dry ingredients and set aside.

3   Whisk milk, egg, and oil in small bowl until frothy and pour into well in dry ingredients. Add corn and stir only enough to combine—specks of flour should be clearly visible in batter.

4   Spoon batter into muffin pans, dividing amount equally—each muffin pan cup will be approximately two-thirds full, though occasionally a bit more or a bit less.

5   Slide onto middle oven shelf and bake 20 to 25 minutes until muffins have risen and their tops are nicely rounded and evenly browned.

6   Serve at once with unsalted butter. Or cool to room temperature before serving. For something a little different, try cooled muffins with Guacamole (page 208) or Salsa (page 212).

EASY ADD-ONS:

TOSS WITH DRY INGREDIENTS BEFORE ADDING COMBINED LIQUIDS:

* ⅓ to ½ cup crumbled crisply cooked bacon

* ⅓ cup moderately finely chopped sun-dried tomatoes: Use dried—not oil-packed—and hydrate. Here's how: Place dried tomatoes in 2-cup oven-proof glass measure, add 1 cup water, cover loosely with plastic wrap, and microwave 3 minutes on Medium (50 percent power). Let stand, still covered, in microwave 5 minutes more. Drain well, pat dry on paper toweling, then chop.

* ¼ cup each crumbled crisply cooked bacon and moderately finely chopped sun-dried tomatoes (see above)

ADD TO COMBINED LIQUIDS BEFORE MIXING INTO DRY INGREDIENTS:

* ¼ cup moderately finely chopped drained and seeded canned jalapeño peppers

* ¼ cup each crumbled crisply cooked bacon and moderately finely chopped drained and seeded canned jalapeño peppers

Henny Penny Muffins

makes about 1 dozen

My good New York friend and colleague Joanne Hayes, who was for years the food editor of *Country Living* magazine, introduced me to Henny Penny Muffins. When I asked about them, Joanne emailed, "I looked everywhere for the recipe I had when I was an eighth-grade home economics teacher in Greenbelt, Maryland, and couldn't find it, so looked online and found several, some of which suggested that it was a recipe from the Civil War."

I, myself, then did a little additional research and discovered, to my surprise, that at least one source attributes the recipe to Laura Ingalls Wilder (1867–1957), and claims that a recipe for Henny Penny Muffins appears in *The Laura Ingalls Wilder Country Cookbook*, a "juvenile cookbook" (for the ten-and-up age group) published in 1995 thanks to a newly discovered cache of Wilder recipes. William T. Anderson (no relation of mine) is listed as coauthor. I haven't seen this book so can't confirm that Henny Penny Muffins actually appear there and, if so, if Wilder created the recipe.

Joanne, who's a painstaking food historian, adds this additional online Henny Penny info: "One person published a recipe that had come from my muffins article in the October 1993 issue of *Country Living* [that predates the Wilder cookbook] so maybe I think of this recipe whenever I think of a muffin collection. I have always thought this a 1940s recipe and that's what I said in my muffins article."

Her version calls for splitting the muffins hot and topping with gravy. "The muffins," she explains, "are supposed to be made out of leftover chicken so there would have been leftover gravy as well."

What follows is my own spin on Henny Penny Muffins in which I substitute stone-ground cornmeal for some of the flour and change all the seasonings. And as Joanne says, this is the recipe to make when you have leftover chicken and gravy. Of course, leftover turkey and turkey gravy work equally well (and check the ham variation below). **Tip:** *To grate onion, lay several sheets of wax paper on the counter, then holding a fine-toothed Microplane on the paper at about a 45-degree angle, briskly rub a small peeled yellow onion back and forth on it. You'll have the amount of finely grated onion you need in less than a minute.*

VARIATION:

Higgy-Piggy Muffins: Prepare as directed, eliminating sage and adding ½ teaspoon allspice and ¼ teaspoon freshly grated nutmeg. Also substitute ½ to ¾ cup coarsely chopped leftover baked or boiled ham for chicken. Serve hot with unsalted butter and/or apple jelly. Or skip the butter and serve with apple butter. Makes about 1 dozen.

1 cup sifted all-purpose flour

1 cup unsifted stone-ground cornmeal (preferably yellow)

2½ teaspoons baking powder

1 teaspoon granulated sugar or raw sugar

½ teaspoon baking soda

½ teaspoon salt

½ teaspoon dried thyme leaves, crumbled

½ teaspoon rubbed sage

¼ teaspoon freshly ground black pepper

1 cup buttermilk (not fat-free)

¼ cup (½ stick) unsalted butter, melted

1 large egg beaten with 3 tablespoons finely grated yellow onion (see Tip, page 92)

½ to ¾ cup moderately coarsely chopped cooked chicken (a 50-50 mix of light and dark meat)

1½ to 2 cups leftover chicken gravy

1 Preheat oven to 400°F. Lightly grease 12 standard-size muffin pan cups or spritz with nonstick cooking spray or, if you prefer, insert a crinkly muffin liner into each cup. Set pans aside.

2 Combine first nine ingredients (flour through black pepper) in medium mixing bowl, make well in center of dry ingredients, and set aside.

3 Whisk buttermilk with butter and egg mixture in small bowl until smooth, then mix in chicken. Pour into well in dry ingredients, and stir only enough to combine—specks of flour should be clearly visible in batter.

4 Spoon batter into muffin pans, dividing amount equally—each muffin pan cup will be approximately two-thirds full, though occasionally a bit more or a bit less.

5 Slide onto middle oven shelf and bake 20 to 25 minutes until muffins have risen and their tops are gently rounded and lightly browned.

6 About 5 minutes before muffins are done, pour gravy into small saucepan, set over low heat, and bring slowly to serving temperature, stirring occasionally.

7 Serve muffins at once, split, and topped with ladlings of gravy. If you have no leftover gravy, serve muffins oven-hot with unsalted butter or softened cream cheese.

Corn Muffins with Blue Cheese and Toasted Pecans

makes about 1 dozen

Even as a little girl I adored blue cheese—not the wimpy blue cheese spreads sold in little glass jars at the supermarket but the "stinky" Danish blues and Roqueforts that my mother would order especially for me. And the "stinkier" the better. My adult favorite is Gorgonzola, particularly Gorgonzola dolce, which most high-end groceries now routinely sell. Unlike the firmer blues, it doesn't crumble so it must be cut into pieces about the size of lentils. I call for toasted pecans in this recipe because their pronounced nuttiness can stand up to the sharpness of any blue cheese. **Note:** *Because of the saltiness of the cheeses, this recipe calls for no additional salt.*

1 cup sifted all-purpose flour

1 cup yellow cornmeal (not stone-ground)

2 tablespoons granulated sugar or raw sugar

2 tablespoons freshly grated Parmigiano-Reggiano

2 teaspoons baking powder

1 teaspoon dried marjoram leaves, crumbled

½ teaspoon dried thyme leaves, crumbled

½ teaspoon baking soda

¼ teaspoon freshly ground black pepper

½ cup coarsely chopped toasted pecans (see page 27)

¼ cup finely diced Gorgonzola dolce or crumbled Roquefort, Danish blue, or Gorgonzola cheese (see headnote)

1 cup buttermilk (not fat-free)

¼ cup (½ stick) unsalted butter, melted

1 large egg, lightly beaten

1 Preheat oven to 400°F. Lightly grease 12 standard-size muffin pan cups or spritz with nonstick cooking spray or, if you prefer, insert a crinkly muffin liner into each cup. Set pans aside.

2 Whisk first nine ingredients (flour through black pepper) together in medium mixing bowl. Add pecans and Gorgonzola, toss to combine, make well in center of dry ingredients, and set aside.

3 Combine buttermilk, butter, and egg in small bowl, beating until smooth. Pour into well in dry ingredients, and stir only enough to combine—specks of flour should be visible in batter.

4 Spoon batter into muffin pans, dividing amount equally—each muffin pan cup will be approximately two-thirds full, though occasionally a bit more or a bit less.

5 Slide onto middle oven shelf and bake 20 to 25 minutes until muffins have risen and their tops are gently rounded and lightly browned.

6 Serve muffins at once with plenty of unsalted butter.

EASY ADD-ONS TO POLENTA MUFFINS ▷
(TOSS WITH DRY INGREDIENTS BEFORE ADDING COMBINED LIQUIDS):

* $1/4$ cup coarsely crumbled crisply cooked bacon. Reduce amount of salt in recipe to $1/4$ teaspoon.

* $1/4$ cup finely chopped prosciutto. Reduce amount of salt in recipe to $1/4$ teaspoon.

* $1/3$ cup coarsely chopped lightly toasted pignoli (pine nuts). For directions on how to toast pine nuts, see page 28.

Polenta Muffins with Parmigiano-Reggiano and Rosemary

makes about 1 dozen

Though *farina di mais* is Italian for "cornmeal," most of us are more familiar with polenta, Italian cornmeal cooked into a creamy carb that's served in place of pasta or potatoes. I've taken a bit of license with this recipe title because what goes into these muffins is not a gruel but plain yellow cornmeal, the granular kind most supermarkets sell. I just like the sound of Polenta Muffins better.

1 cup sifted all-purpose flour

1 cup yellow cornmeal (see headnote)

⅓ cup freshly grated Parmigiano-Reggiano

1 tablespoon baking powder

2 teaspoons sugar

½ teaspoon salt

½ teaspoon finely chopped fresh rosemary or ¼ teaspoon dried rosemary leaves, crumbled

¼ teaspoon freshly ground black pepper

1 cup milk

1 large egg

¼ cup extra-virgin olive oil

1 Preheat oven to 400°F. Lightly grease 12 standard-size muffin pan cups or spritz with nonstick cooking spray or, if you prefer, insert a crinkly muffin liner into each cup. Set pans aside.

2 Combine first eight ingredients (flour through black pepper) in medium mixing bowl, make well in center of dry ingredients, and set aside.

3 Whisk milk with egg and oil in small bowl until frothy, pour into well in dry ingredients, and stir only enough to combine—specks of flour should be visible in batter.

4 Spoon batter into muffin pans, dividing amount equally—each muffin pan cup will be approximately two-thirds full, though occasionally a bit more or a bit less.

5 Slide onto middle oven shelf and bake 20 to 25 minutes until muffins have risen and their tops are nicely rounded and evenly browned.

6 Serve at once with unsalted butter or softened cream cheese.

Corn Muffins with Wild Mushrooms

makes about
1 dozen

For some time now I've been trying to develop a recipe for mushroom muffins and after considerable trial and error, now know that fresh mushrooms, even when sautéed, lose all flavor when baked into muffins. Then, cruising supermarket aisles one day, I came upon little packets of dried mushrooms and I thought, "Bingo!" Their intense flavor would surely survive 20 minutes or so in a hot oven. But their leathery texture presented a problem. So I simmered them 15 minutes in water, drained them, and saved their cooking liquid. Worked beautifully. So which mushrooms are best for this recipe? My own choice would be porcini.

¾ ounce dried porcini mushrooms (about ¾ to 1 cup loosely packed)

1 cup water

1 cup sifted all-purpose flour

1 cup yellow cornmeal (not stone-ground)

1 tablespoon baking powder

1 tablespoon raw sugar

¾ teaspoon salt (½ teaspoon if you use bacon drippings)

½ teaspoon dried thyme leaves, crumbled

¼ teaspoon freshly ground black pepper

¾ cup milk (about)

1 large egg

¼ cup melted unsalted butter, bacon drippings, or corn oil

1 Preheat oven to 400°F. Simmer mushrooms in water in uncovered small saucepan over low heat 15 minutes until soft.

2 Meanwhile, lightly grease 12 standard-size muffin pan cups or spritz with nonstick cooking spray or, if you prefer, insert a crinkly muffin liner into each cup. Set pans aside.

3 Combine next seven ingredients (flour through black pepper) in medium mixing bowl. Make well in center and set aside.

4 Using slotted spoon, lift mushrooms to sieve and rinse with cold water to remove any grit and sand; drain well and chop fairly fine. Pour mushroom liquid through cheesecloth-lined fine sieve into spouted 1-cup measure, and add enough milk to total 1 cup.

5 Whisk milk mixture with egg and butter in small bowl until frothy and add chopped mushrooms. Pour into well in dry ingredients and stir only enough to combine—specks of flour should be visible in batter.

6 Spoon batter into muffin pans, dividing amount equally—each muffin pan cup will be approximately two-thirds full, though occasionally a bit more or a bit less.

7 Slide onto middle oven shelf and bake 20 to 25 minutes until muffins have risen and their tops are nicely rounded and evenly browned.

8 Serve at once with unsalted butter or softened cream cheese. Or, if you prefer, cool muffins to room temperature before serving.

Easy Jalapeño Corn Muffins

makes about 1 dozen

This is my riff on old-timey corn muffins, the kind Southerners love made with stone-ground white cornmeal. Your supermarket doesn't sell stone-ground meal? You can order it online (see Sources, page 220). **Note:** *To enrich the flavor of these corn muffins, I use melted bacon drippings as the shortening. Every frugal cook—count me among them—keeps a little jar of drippings left over from frying bacon. Tightly capped and stored in the refrigerator, it keeps for several months. I also use it when stir-frying collards and turnip or mustard greens. If you use bacon drippings for this recipe, their saltiness eliminates the need for additional salt. But if you use melted unsalted butter, you'll need to add about ¹/₂ teaspoon salt.*

1 cup sifted all-purpose flour

1 cup unsifted stone-ground cornmeal (white or yellow)

2 tablespoons sugar

2¹/₂ teaspoons baking powder

¹/₂ teaspoon baking soda

¹/₄ teaspoon ground hot red pepper (cayenne)

1 cup buttermilk (not fat-free)

1 large egg

¹/₄ cup melted bacon drippings or unsalted butter plus ¹/₂ teaspoon salt (see Note above)

2 tablespoons finely chopped cored seeded fresh jalapeños or well drained canned jalapeños

1 Preheat oven to 400°F. Lightly grease 12 standard-size muffin pan cups or spritz with nonstick cooking spray or, if you prefer, insert a crinkly muffin liner into each cup. Set pans aside.

2 Combine first six ingredients (flour through cayenne) in medium mixing bowl, make well in center of dry ingredients, and set aside.

3 Beat buttermilk, egg, and bacon drippings in second medium bowl until smooth, then mix in jalapeños. Pour into well in dry ingredients and stir only enough to combine—you should see specks of flour in batter.

4 Spoon batter into muffin pans, dividing amount equally—each muffin pan cup will be approximately two-thirds full, though occasionally a bit more or a bit less.

5 Slide onto middle oven shelf and bake 20 to 25 minutes until muffins have risen and their tops are gently rounded and lightly browned.

6 Serve at once with plenty of unsalted butter. Or cool to room temperature before serving.

EASY ADD-ONS:

TOSS WITH DRY INGREDIENTS BEFORE ADDING COMBINED LIQUIDS. NOTE: EVEN IF USING UNSALTED BUTTER, YOU WILL NOT NEED TO ADD ANY SALT BECAUSE THESE ADD-ONS ARE QUITE SALTY.

* ½ cup coarsely shredded sharp Cheddar cheese

* ¼ cup freshly grated Parmigiano-Reggiano

* ¼ cup coarsely crumbled crisply cooked bacon

* ¼ cup each freshly grated Parmigiano-Reggiano and coarsely crumbled crisply cooked bacon

ADD TO COMBINED LIQUIDS BEFORE MIXING INTO DRY INGREDIENTS:

* ½ cup well drained thawed frozen whole-kernel corn

Peppery Pico de Gallo Corn Muffins

makes about 1 dozen

Ever since I first tasted pico de gallo—years ago at Cafe Pasqual's, my favorite Santa Fe restaurant—I've been fascinated by its variations and versatility. You can make your own, of course (see page 213). But to save time, use a bottled one sold at some supermarkets and failing that, something from the eye-popping array of salsas (even more salsas are available online; see Sources, page 220). I've even been known to substitute diced tomatoes with green chilies (Ro-Tel). All's well as long as your muffins are both colorful and flavorful. **Note:** *If you use bacon drippings in this recipe, you might want to eliminate the salt because the pico de gallo and drippings are both pretty salty.*

1¼ cups yellow cornmeal (not stone-ground)

¾ cup sifted all-purpose flour

2 teaspoons baking powder

½ teaspoon baking soda

¼ teaspoon salt (see Note above)

¼ teaspoon freshly ground black pepper

1 cup well-drained canned pico de gallo, tomato salsa, or canned diced tomatoes and green chiles (see headnote)

½ cup tomato or tomato-vegetable juice

3 tablespoons vegetable oil or melted bacon drippings

1 large egg, lightly beaten

1 Preheat oven to 400°F. Lightly grease 12 standard-size muffin pan cups or spritz with nonstick cooking spray or, if you prefer, insert a crinkly muffin liner into each cup. Set pans aside.

2 Combine first six ingredients (corn-meal through black pepper) in medium mixing bowl, make well in center of dry ingredients, and set aside.

3 Mix pico de gallo, tomato juice, oil, and egg in second medium bowl, pour into well in dry ingredients, and stir only enough to combine—specks of flour should be visible in batter.

4 Spoon batter into muffin pans, dividing amount equally—each muffin pan cup will be approximately two-thirds full, though occasionally a bit more or a bit less.

5 Slide onto middle oven shelf and bake 20 to 25 minutes until muffins have risen and their tops are slightly rounded and evenly browned.

6 Serve warm with Guacamole (page 208). Good, too, with softened cream cheese or bean dip.

VARIATION:

Green Chili Muffins: Prepare as directed, substituting a good bottled salsa verde for pico de gallo and vegetable or chicken broth for tomato juice. Makes about 1 dozen.

Mexicali Muffins

makes about 1 dozen

These corn muffins contain a bit of masa harina (taco/tortilla flour), which is nothing more than finely ground dried hominy. And hominy? Corn kernels given a lye bath till they puff and their skins pop off. These confetti-bright muffins also contain lightly sautéed scallions and red and green bell peppers. The peppers, you'll be pleased to know, can be cooked ahead of time and refrigerated until you're ready to use them. It's a good idea, however, to let them come to room temperature before mixing them into the muffin batter, which takes about 15 minutes. **Note:** *If you have no masa harina on hand and can't find a small bag of it (my supermarkets only carry five-pound bags), omit the masa and use 1 cup yellow cornmeal.*

¼ cup corn oil or vegetable oil

4 large scallions, trimmed and coarsely chopped (include some green tops)

⅓ cup coarsely chopped cored seeded red bell pepper (about ½ medium)

⅓ cup coarsely chopped cored seeded green bell pepper (about ½ medium)

1 teaspoon dried Mexican oregano leaves, crumbled

1 cup sifted all-purpose flour

¾ cup yellow cornmeal (not stone-ground)

¼ cup unsifted masa harina (see Note above)

1 tablespoon raw sugar

2 teaspoons baking powder

½ teaspoon baking soda

½ teaspoon salt

¼ teaspoon freshly ground black pepper

1 cup buttermilk (not fat-free)

1 large egg

1 Preheat oven to 400°F. Lightly grease 12 standard-size muffin pan cups or spritz with nonstick cooking spray or, if you prefer, insert a crinkly muffin liner into each cup. Set pans aside.

2 Heat oil in small heavy skillet over moderately high heat until ripples appear on pan bottom—about 1 minute. Add scallions, red and green bell peppers, and oregano and stir-fry just until vegetables are limp and golden—2 to 3 minutes. Remove from heat and reserve.

3 Whisk together next eight ingredients (flour through black pepper) in medium bowl, make well in center of dry ingredients, and set aside.

4 In second medium bowl, beat buttermilk and egg until smooth, add reserved skillet mixture and stir well. Pour buttermilk mixture into well in dry ingredients and stir only enough to mix—specks of flour should be clearly visible.

5 Spoon batter into muffin pans, dividing amount equally—each muffin pan cup will be approximately two-thirds full, though occasionally a bit more or a bit less.

6 Slide onto middle oven shelf and bake 20 to 25 minutes until muffins have risen and their tops are gently rounded and lightly browned.

7 Serve at once with plenty of unsalted butter. Or cool to room temperature before serving and serve with Guacamole (page 208) or Salsa (page 212).

More Muffin Recipes
Containing Cornmeal
That Can Be Found
Elsewhere in This Book:

* Benne Muffins Variation (page 53)

* Brown Bread Muffins (page 133)

* Herb Garden Muffins Variation
  (page 40)

* Multi-Grain Muffins (page 118)

* Smoky Country Ham and Cheese
  Muffins Variation (page 54)

Nutritious WHOLE-Grain Muffins

The easiest way to add whole grains to your diet, the most delicious, and the fastest, is simply to whip up a batch of muffins using whole-wheat flour, rye flour, indeed almost any grain that's milled into a flour that's neither "refined" nor sifted.

But, make a note: If a muffin recipe calls for 2 cups sifted all-purpose flour, you should substitute whole-grain flour for only part of the all-purpose, usually ³⁄₄ to 1 cup—*unsifted* because you don't want to lose the bits of husk and germ that add texture and nutrients.

Take whole-wheat flour. It contains more than twice the amount of calcium of all-purpose flour, nearly four times the phosphorus and potassium, not to mention five times the amount of fiber. Moreover, 1 cup unsifted whole-wheat flour weighs in at fifty fewer calories than 1 cup all-purpose. So why not use 100 percent whole-grain flour instead of a 50-50 combo with all-purpose flour? Because those muffins would be leaden.

Of course, there are other effective ways to boost the nutritional heft of muffins: adding rolled oats (oatmeal), bran, or wheat germ, as well as nuts or fruits or any one of countless combinations. Nor would it be amiss to add a bit of meat and/or cheese to whole-grain muffins as long as the flavors are compatible. Finally, you can boost the nutritional value of a muffin simply by using a combination of flours because the vitamin and mineral contents vary from wheat to rye to oats to corn with one grain often providing the nutrients others lack.

Mindful of this, I've assembled the best muffin recipes I could find for this chapter, some of them old classics, some of them entirely original. So in the pages that follow you'll find things like Not Your Mama's Carrot Muffins . . . Whole-Wheat Mustard Muffins with Cheddar and Country Ham . . . Honeyed Whole-Wheat English Muffins . . . Oatmeal-Applesauce Muffins . . . Brown Bread Muffins . . . Old-Fashioned Rye Muffins . . . Crunchy Wheat Germ Muffins and more. I hope you like them.

Whole-Wheat Muffins

makes about
1 dozen

These muffins are every bit as easy as Entry-Level Muffins (page 34), equally versatile but more mineral- and vitamin-packed.

1 cup sifted all-purpose flour

³⁄₄ cup unsifted whole-wheat flour

2 tablespoons granulated sugar or raw sugar

1 tablespoon baking powder

1 teaspoon salt

¹⁄₂ teaspoon freshly grated nutmeg

1 cup milk

¹⁄₄ cup vegetable oil

1 large egg, well beaten with 1 tablespoon molasses (not too dark)

1 Preheat oven to 400°F. Lightly grease 12 standard-size muffin pan cups or spritz with nonstick cooking spray or, if you prefer, insert a crinkly muffin liner into each cup. Set pans aside.

2 Combine first six ingredients (all-purpose flour through nutmeg) in medium mixing bowl, make well in center of dry ingredients, and set aside.

3 Whisk milk with oil and egg mixture in small bowl until smooth, pour into well in dry ingredients, and stir only enough to combine—bits of flour should be clearly visible.

4 Spoon batter into muffin pans, dividing amount equally—each muffin pan cup will be approximately two-thirds full, though occasionally a bit more or a bit less.

5 Slide onto middle oven shelf and bake about 20 to 25 minutes until muffins have risen and their tops are nicely rounded and evenly browned.

6 Serve hot with plenty of unsalted butter and a favorite jam or jelly. I also like these muffins with Maple Butter (page 216).

VARIATIONS:

Whole-Wheat Muffins with Raisins: Prepare as directed but add $\frac{1}{2}$ to $\frac{2}{3}$ cup dark seedless raisins (or, if you prefer, dried currants) to combined dry ingredients and toss well. Make well in center of dry ingredients, then follow steps 3 through 6 to complete recipe. Makes about 1 dozen.

Whole-Wheat Muffins with Dried Cranberries: Prepare as directed but add $\frac{1}{2}$ to $\frac{2}{3}$ cup dried cranberries (or, if you prefer, dried blueberries) to combined dry ingredients and toss well. Make well in center of dry ingredients, then follow steps 3 through 6 to complete recipe. Makes about 1 dozen.

Whole-Wheat Muffins with Black Walnuts: Prepare as directed but add $\frac{1}{2}$ to $\frac{2}{3}$ cup coarsely chopped black walnuts (or, if you prefer, English walnuts, pecans, or wild hickory nuts) to combined dry ingredients and toss well. Make well in center of dry ingredients, then follow steps 3 through 6 to complete recipe. Makes about 1 dozen.

Blueberry Whole-Wheat Muffins

makes about 1 dozen

There are blueberry muffins and blueberry muffins but few as good as these made with whole-wheat flour. If fresh blueberries are out of season, use the frozen—solidly frozen. They work just fine.

1 cup sifted all-purpose flour

1 cup unsifted whole-wheat flour

⅓ cup granulated sugar or raw sugar

1 tablespoon baking powder

¼ teaspoon salt

½ cup coarsely chopped toasted pecans (see page 27)

1 cup milk

¼ cup (½ stick) unsalted butter, melted

1 large egg, lightly beaten with 1 teaspoon finely grated orange zest

1 cup fresh or solidly frozen blueberries

1 Preheat oven to 400°F. Lightly grease 12 standard-size muffin pan cups or spritz with nonstick cooking spray or, if you prefer, insert a crinkly muffin liner into each cup. Set pans aside.

2 Combine first five ingredients (all-purpose flour through salt) in medium mixing bowl. Add pecans, toss well, then make well in center of dry ingredients and set aside.

3 Whisk milk, butter, and egg mixture in small bowl until smooth, then mix in blueberries. Pour into well in dry ingredients, and stir only enough to combine—specks of flour should be visible in batter.

4 Spoon batter into muffin pans, dividing amount equally—each muffin pan cup will be approximately two-thirds full, though occasionally a bit more or a bit less.

5 Slide onto middle oven shelf and bake 20 to 25 minutes until muffins have risen and their tops are nicely rounded and evenly browned.

6 Serve oven-hot with plenty of unsalted butter. I also like these muffins with Maple Butter (page 216).

Whole-Wheat Mustard Muffins with Cheddar and Country Ham

makes about 2 dozen

These unusual muffins come from my good friend Karen Barker, one of this country's most creative pastry chefs and until recently co-owner with her husband, Chef Ben Barker, of Durham's beloved Magnolia Grill, which they recently shuttered after twenty-five years. Both Barkers and their restaurant have won armloads of prestigious national awards and surely deserve a little time off. Their next move? Relaxing, spending time with family, traveling, tasting. When I asked Karen if she had a favorite muffin recipe that she'd be willing to share, this recipe came back by return email along with this note: "I thought you'd have a bunch of sweet muffin recipes, so for something a little different I've attached a version for a savory one. I used to make them occasionally for brunch at Fearrington House [the Pittsboro, North Carolina inn where Karen and Ben worked soon after graduating from The Culinary Institute of America]. I would suggest serving these with soft scrambled eggs or tomato soup. I don't usually butter them (unless I'm splitting and toasting the leftovers) although that certainly wouldn't be a bad thing to do. They are pretty moist and flavorful on their own but try them and see what you think." This recipe makes twice as many muffins as the other recipes in this book, but they're so unusual, so delicious, I decided to go with the full amount. Just freeze the extra muffins, then reheat before serving (see About Reheating Muffins, page 15).

2 cups sifted all-purpose flour

2 cups unsifted whole-wheat flour

2 tablespoons baking powder

1 tablespoon sugar

1 teaspoon kosher salt

½ cup finely chopped fully cooked country ham or finely chopped unsliced prosciutto or Serrano ham

1 cup moderately coarsely shredded sharp Cheddar cheese

3 medium scallions, trimmed and finely chopped (include some green tops)

3 large eggs

2 cups milk

2 tablespoons Dijon mustard

2 tablespoons coarse grainy mustard

¾ cup (1½ sticks) unsalted butter, melted and cooled slightly

½ teaspoon hot red pepper sauce

1 Preheat oven to 350°F. Lightly grease 24 standard-size muffin pan cups or spritz with nonstick cooking spray or, if you prefer, insert a crinkly muffin liner into each cup. Set pans aside.

2 Whisk first five ingredients (all-purpose flour through salt) in large mixing bowl until well combined. Add ham, cheese, and scallions, toss well, make well in center of dry ingredients, and set aside.

3 Whisk remaining ingredients in second large bowl until frothy, pour into well in dry ingredients, and stir only enough to combine—specks of flour should be visible in batter.

4 Spoon batter into muffin pans, dividing amount equally— each muffin pan cup will be approximately two-thirds full, though occasionally a bit more or a bit less.

5 Slide onto middle oven shelf and bake 30 to 35 minutes until muffins have risen and their tops are nicely rounded and lightly browned.

6 Remove muffins from oven, cool in pans 10 minutes, then remove and serve warm with or without unsalted butter.

Multi-Grain Muffins

With more and more of us becoming health conscious, there's every reason to load muffins with whole grains and to minimize the amount of sugar. These measure up and are just the thing for breakfast either as traditional muffins or as muffin tops. **Tip:** *To get a jump on the morning meal, you can combine all the dry ingredients the night before. I simply place the first ten ingredients (all-purpose flour through salt) in a plastic zipper bag, give them a good shake, seal, and refrigerate overnight.*

1 cup sifted all-purpose flour

⅓ cup unsifted whole-wheat flour

⅓ cup quick-cooking rolled oats (oatmeal)

¼ cup yellow cornmeal (not stone-ground)

2 tablespoons bran cereal (not flakes)

2 tablespoons wheat germ

2 tablespoons raw sugar

2½ teaspoons baking powder

½ teaspoon baking soda

¼ teaspoon salt

½ cup coarsely chopped pecans

½ cup dark seedless raisins or dried currants

1 cup buttermilk (not fat-free)

¼ cup (½ stick) unsalted butter, melted

3 tablespoons molasses (not too dark)

1 large egg

1 Preheat oven to 400°F. Lightly grease 12 standard-size muffin pan cups or 12 muffin top cups or spritz with non-stick cooking spray. If you're baking standard-size muffins, you might prefer to insert a crinkly muffin liner into each cup. Set pans aside.

2 Combine first ten ingredients (all-purpose flour through salt) in medium mixing bowl. Add pecans and raisins, toss well, then make well in center of dry ingredients and set aside.

3 Whisk buttermilk, butter, molasses, and egg in small bowl until smooth. Pour into well in dry ingredients, and stir only enough to combine—specks of flour should be visible in batter.

4 Spoon batter into muffin pans, dividing amount equally—each standard-size muffin pan cup will be approximately two-thirds full, though occasionally a bit more or a bit less. If using muffin top pans, spread batter to edge of each cup, if necessary.

5 Slide onto middle oven shelf and bake standard-size muffins 20 to 25 minutes and muffin tops 10 to 12 minutes—in either case until risen, nicely rounded, and evenly browned.

6 Serve oven-hot with plenty of unsalted butter. These muffins are particularly good with Maple Butter (page 216).

Not Your Mama's Carrot Muffins

Once again, I'm trimming the amount of sugar that goes into many carrot muffin recipes and boosting their nutritional value with whole-wheat flour. And instead of the usual cinnamon and allspice to season, I'm using fresh ginger and lemongrass. And substituting coconut milk for milk. Every supermarket now carries cans of coconut milk—look for it in the "international" section. A friend who tried this recipe said these were equally delicious baked as muffins or muffin tops, so I give baking times for both. **Tip:** *The fastest way to grate fresh ginger? On a fine-toothed Microplane.* **Note:** *For Classic Carrot Muffins, see page 147.*

1 cup sifted all-purpose flour

1 cup unsifted whole-wheat flour

1/4 cup raw sugar

2 1/2 teaspoons baking powder

1/4 teaspoon salt

3/4 cup coarsely chopped unsalted dry-roasted peanuts or macadamia nuts

1 1/4 cups canned coconut milk (not low-fat)

3 tablespoons peanut oil or vegetable oil blended with 1 tablespoon Thai peanut sauce and 1 teaspoon Asian toasted sesame oil

1 large egg, lightly beaten with 1 teaspoon finely grated lemon zest

1 tablespoon finely grated fresh ginger (see Tip above)

1 tablespoon very finely minced lemongrass (inner white stalk only)

1 cup coarsely grated tender young carrots (about 3 small)

1   Preheat oven to 400°F. Lightly grease 12 standard-size muffin pan cups or spritz with nonstick cooking spray, or insert a crinkly muffin liner into each cup. Or, if you prefer, spritz 12 muffin top pan cups with nonstick cooking spray. Set pans aside.

2   Combine first five ingredients (all-purpose flour through salt) in medium mixing bowl. Set aside ¼ cup peanuts add remaining peanuts to bowl, and toss well. Make well in center of dry ingredients and set aside.

3   Whisk next five ingredients (coconut milk through lemongrass) in second medium bowl until well blended, then mix in carrots. Pour into well in dry ingredients, and stir only enough to combine—specks of flour should be visible in batter.

4   Spoon batter into muffin or muffin top pans, dividing amount equally. Sprinkle ¼ cup reserved peanuts evenly on top of muffins or muffin tops.

5   Slide onto middle oven shelf and bake muffins 20 to 25 minutes and muffin tops 10 to 12 minutes, until their tops are nicely rounded and evenly browned.

6   Serve oven-hot with plenty of unsalted butter. Delicious, too, with Lemon Curd (page 214) or ginger marmalade—no butter needed.

Upside-Down Pineapple-Carrot Muffins

makes about 1 dozen

A little fancier than Classic Carrot Muffins (page 147), these are perfect for a brunch or special breakfast. They're easy but—make a note—they should be baked in well buttered or spritzed muffin pans. Do not use crinkly paper liners because they'll soak up the pineapple mixture in the bottom of each muffin pan cup.

1 (8-ounce) can crushed pineapple in 100% pineapple juice, well drained and liquid reserved

⅓ cup plus 2 tablespoons firmly packed light brown sugar

1 cup sifted all-purpose flour

1 cup unsifted whole-wheat flour

2 teaspoons baking powder

1 teaspoon ground cinnamon

½ teaspoon baking soda

½ teaspoon ground ginger

½ teaspoon ground allspice

¼ teaspoon salt

¾ cup coarsely chopped pecans or walnuts

1 (5-ounce) can evaporated milk (not low-fat or fat-free) plus enough reserved pineapple juice and water, if needed, to total 1 cup liquid

¼ cup (½ stick) unsalted butter, melted, or ¼ cup vegetable oil

1 large egg

1 cup coarsely grated tender young carrots (about 3 small)

1 Preheat oven to 400°F. Butter 12 standard-size muffin pan cups well or spritz with nonstick cooking spray. Combine $\frac{1}{2}$ cup drained canned pineapple with 2 tablespoons of the sugar and spoon into muffin pan cups, dividing amount evenly. Set pans aside.

2 Combine the remaining $\frac{1}{3}$ cup sugar with next eight ingredients (all-purpose flour through salt) in medium mixing bowl. Add pecans, toss well, then make well in center of dry ingredients and set aside.

3 Whisk milk mixture, butter, and egg in second medium bowl until smooth, then mix in remaining crushed pineapple and carrots. Pour into well in dry ingredients, and stir only enough to combine—specks of flour should be visible in batter.

4 Spoon batter into muffin pans, dividing amount equally—each muffin pan cup will be approximately two-thirds full, though occasionally a bit more or a bit less.

5 Slide onto middle oven shelf and bake 20 to 25 minutes until muffins have risen and their tops are nicely rounded and evenly browned.

6 Loosen each muffin around edge with small thin-blade spatula, then arrange bottoms-up on large heated plate.

7 Serve hot with plenty of unsalted butter or with pineapple preserves if you prefer.

Crunchy Wheat Germ Muffins

makes about 1 dozen

I've always liked the nutty flavor and crunchiness of wheat germ, not to mention its nutritional value: hefty amounts of thiamine (B_1), riboflavin (B_2), iron, phosphorus, and potassium. Unfortunately, wheat germ's oiliness makes it turn rancid fairly fast, but if stored in the freezer, it lasts several months. **Tip:** *Prepare the topping first so it's ready to use as soon as the batter's in the pan.*

Topping:

3 tablespoons wheat germ

1 tablespoon freshly grated Parmigiano-Reggiano

1 tablespoon melted unsalted butter

2 teaspoons raw sugar

Muffins:

1½ cups unsifted all-purpose flour

1 cup wheat germ

¼ cup freshly grated Parmigiano-Reggiano

1 tablespoon raw sugar

½ teaspoon salt

½ teaspoon dried marjoram leaves, crumbled

¼ teaspoon dried thyme leaves, crumbled

1 cup milk

¼ cup vegetable oil

1 large egg

1 Preheat oven to 400°F. Lightly grease 12 standard-size muffin pan cups or spritz with nonstick cooking spray or, if you prefer, insert a crinkly muffin liner into each cup. Set pans aside.

2 **Topping:** Combine all ingredients in small bowl; set aside.

3 **Muffins:** Combine first seven ingredients (flour through thyme) in medium mixing bowl, make well in center of dry ingredients, and set aside.

4 Whisk milk with oil and egg in small bowl until smooth. Pour into well in dry ingredients, and stir only enough to combine—bits of flour should be clearly visible in batter.

5 Spoon batter into muffin pans, dividing amount equally— each muffin pan cup will be approximately two-thirds full, though occasionally a bit more or a bit less. Sprinkle topping evenly over each muffin.

6 Slide onto middle oven shelf and bake about 20 minutes until muffins have risen and their tops are nicely rounded and evenly browned.

7 Serve hot with plenty of unsalted butter and jam.

Classic Bran Muffins

makes about
1 dozen

Even more vitamin- and mineral-packed than Whole-Wheat Muffins (page 112), bran muffins are excellent sources of nearly all the B vitamins as well as fair sources of vitamins A, C, and D. Moreover, their fiber content is way up there. Ditto their iron, manganese, magnesium, calcium, and phosphorus. So enjoy with a clear conscience. And an even clearer conscience if you can hold the butter.

1¼ cups bran cereal (not flakes)

1 cup milk

1¼ cups sifted all-purpose flour

¼ cup raw sugar or light brown sugar (do not pack)

1 tablespoon baking powder

½ teaspoon salt

½ teaspoon freshly grated nutmeg

¼ teaspoon ground ginger

¼ cup vegetable oil

1 large egg

1 Preheat oven to 425°F. Line 12 standard-size muffin pan cups with crinkly liners and set pans aside.

2 Place bran cereal in small bowl, add milk, and soak 3 minutes. Meanwhile, combine next six ingredients (flour through ginger) in medium bowl, make well in center of dry ingredients, and set aside.

3 Whisk oil and egg in small bowl until frothy, then mix into bran mixture. Pour into well in dry ingredients and stir only enough to combine—bits of flour should be visible in batter.

4 Spoon batter into muffin pans, dividing amount equally— each muffin pan cup will be approximately two-thirds full, though occasionally a bit more or a bit less.

5 Slide onto middle oven shelf and bake 20 to 25 minutes until muffins have risen and their tops are nicely rounded and evenly browned.

6 Serve hot with plenty of unsalted butter and a favorite jam or jelly.

VARIATIONS:

Raisin-Bran Muffins: Prepare step 1 as directed. In step 2 before making well in combined dry ingredients, add ¾ cup dark seedless raisins or dried currants, and toss well. Make well in center of dry ingredients, then follow steps 3 through 6 to complete recipe. Makes about 1 dozen.

Nut-Bran Muffins: Prepare step 1 as directed. In step 2 before making well in combined dry ingredients, add ¾ cup finely chopped pecans, walnuts, black walnuts, or wild hickory nuts, and toss well. Make well in center of dry ingredients, then follow steps 3 through 6 to complete recipe. Makes about 1 dozen.

Berry-Bran Muffins: Prepare step 1 as directed. In step 2 before making well in combined dry ingredients, add ¾ cup dried cranberries or blueberries, and toss well. Make well in center of dry ingredients, then follow steps 3 through 6 to complete recipe. Makes about 1 dozen.

Black Walnut–Bran Muffins

makes about 1½ dozen

Black walnut trees grow wild over much of the South, Midwest, and Great Plains and their nuts taste nothing like the more familiar English walnuts. They're sweeter but what makes them unique is their slightly earthy—dare I say musky?—flavor. Black walnuts are the devil to crack and extracting their meat requires the patience of Job. Fortunately, shelled black walnuts can be ordered online (see Sources, page 220).

2½ cups bran cereal (not flakes)

1⅓ cups milk

2 cups sifted all-purpose flour

¼ cup granulated sugar or raw sugar

1½ teaspoons baking soda

¼ teaspoon salt

⅔ cup coarsely chopped black walnuts, hickory nuts, or pecans

⅔ cup molasses (not too dark)

1 large egg beaten with ¼ cup vegetable oil until frothy

1 Preheat oven to 400°F. Grease 18 standard-size muffin pan cups, spritz with nonstick cooking spray, or insert a crinkly muffin liner into each cup. Set pans aside.

2 Place bran cereal in small bowl, add milk, and let stand 5 minutes. Meanwhile, combine flour, sugar, soda, and salt in medium mixing bowl. Add walnuts and toss well. Make well in center of dry ingredients and set aside.

3 Stir molasses into bran mixture along with egg mixture. Pour into well in dry ingredients and mix only enough to combine; flecks of flour should be visible in batter.

4 Spoon batter into muffin pans, dividing amount equally— each muffin pan cup will be approximately two-thirds full, though occasionally a bit more or a bit less.

5 Slide onto middle oven shelf and bake 20 to 25 minutes until muffins have risen and their tops are nicely rounded and evenly browned.

6 Serve hot with plenty of unsalted butter, softened cream cheese, or Maple Butter (page 216).

Old-Fashioned Rye Muffins

makes about 1 dozen

Pumpernickel fans will love these muffins. And how much easier they are to make than pumpernickel bread. **Note:** *Many high-end supermarkets sell rye flour and it's also available online (see Sources, page 220).* **Tip:** *To intensify the flavor of caraway seeds, heat them a minute or so in a small dry skillet over moderate heat, shaking constantly.*

1 cup sifted all-purpose flour

1 cup unsifted dark rye flour (see Note above)

¼ cup raw sugar

2 teaspoons baking powder

½ teaspoon baking soda

1 teaspoon caraway seeds, lightly crushed (see Tip above)

½ teaspoon salt

1 cup moderately coarsely chopped walnuts, black walnuts, or pecans (optional)

1 cup buttermilk (not fat-free)

¼ cup vegetable oil

2 tablespoons molasses (not too dark)

1 large egg

1 Preheat oven to 400°F. Lightly grease 12 standard-size muffin pan cups, spritz with nonstick cooking spray, or insert a crinkly muffin liner into each cup. Set pans aside.

2 Combine first seven ingredients (all-purpose flour through salt) in medium mixing bowl. Add walnuts, if using, and toss well. Make well in center of dry ingredients and set aside.

3 Whisk buttermilk, oil, molasses, and egg in small bowl until smooth, pour into well in dry ingredients, and stir only enough to combine—specks of flour should be visible in batter.

4 Spoon batter into muffin pans, dividing amount equally—each muffin pan cup will be approximately two-thirds full, though occasionally a bit more or a bit less.

5 Slide onto middle oven shelf and bake 20 to 25 minutes until muffins have risen and their tops are nicely rounded and evenly browned.

6 Serve oven-hot with plenty of unsalted butter or, if you prefer, softened cream cheese.

Brown Bread Muffins

makes about 1 dozen

My mother adored Boston brown bread, and the rattle of Rumford Baking Powder tins in which the batter steamed for hours in a giant kettle is a sound I'll never forget. Is there any reason, I wondered, why those ingredients can't be mixed zip-quick into a muffin batter that bakes for less than half an hour? None at all.

⅔ cup sifted all-purpose flour

⅔ cup unsifted dark rye flour

⅔ cup yellow cornmeal (not stone-ground)

1½ teaspoons baking powder

¾ teaspoon baking soda

½ teaspoon salt

½ cup dark seedless raisins or dried currants

1¼ cups buttermilk (not fat-free)

¼ cup molasses (not too dark)

¼ cup (½ stick) unsalted butter, melted

1 large egg

1 Preheat oven to 400°F. Lightly grease 12 standard-size muffin pan cups or spritz with nonstick cooking spray or, if you prefer, insert a crinkly muffin liner into each cup. Set pans aside.

2 Whisk first six ingredients (all-purpose flour through salt) together in medium mixing bowl. Add raisins, toss well, then make well in center of dry ingredients and set aside.

3 Whisk buttermilk, molasses, butter, and egg in small bowl until smooth, pour into well in dry ingredients, and stir only enough to mix. Specks of flour should be visible in batter.

4 Spoon batter into muffin pans, dividing amount equally— each muffin pan cup will be approximately two-thirds full, though occasionally a bit more or a bit less.

5 Slide onto middle oven shelf and bake 20 to 25 minutes until muffins have risen and their tops are gently rounded.

6 Serve at once with plenty of unsalted butter and, if you like, a favorite jam, jelly, or marmalade.

Oatmeal-Applesauce Muffins

makes about 14 muffins

As with Applesauce Muffins (page 152), homemade applesauce is the applesauce to use, preferably unsweetened or only lightly so. I'm not saying that commercially bottled applesauce won't work. It will, but the muffins won't be as flavorful. **Tip:** *The implement to use for grating the ginger is a fine-toothed Microplane. I pour the evaporated milk into a small bowl, lay the Microplane across the rim, then whisk the peeled ginger back and forth across it a couple of times, letting the shreds fall into the milk. No matter if there's a bit too much—or too little.*

1¾ cups sifted all-purpose flour

¾ cup quick-cooking rolled oats (oatmeal)

¼ cup firmly packed light brown sugar

2 teaspoons baking powder

1 teaspoon baking soda

1 teaspoon ground cinnamon

½ teaspoon freshly grated nutmeg

¼ teaspoon salt

1 cup unsweetened applesauce (see headnote)

1 (5-ounce) can evaporated milk (not low-fat or fat-free), beaten with 1 tablespoon finely grated fresh ginger (see Tip above)

1 large egg

3 tablespoons vegetable oil or melted unsalted butter

1 Preheat oven to 400°F. Lightly grease 14 standard-size muffin pan cups or spritz with nonstick cooking spray or, if you prefer, insert a crinkly muffin liner into each cup. Set pans aside.

2 Whisk first eight ingredients (flour through salt) together in medium mixing bowl. Make well in center and set aside.

3 Combine applesauce, milk mixture, egg, and oil in a second medium bowl, beating until smooth. Pour into well in dry ingredients and stir only enough to mix. Specks of flour should be visible in batter.

4 Spoon batter into muffin pans, dividing amount equally—each muffin pan cup will be approximately two-thirds full, though occasionally a bit more or a bit less.

5 Slide onto middle oven shelf and bake 20 to 25 minutes until muffins have risen and their tops are gently rounded and lightly browned.

6 Serve at once with plenty of unsalted butter and, if you like, apple butter or apple jelly.

Oat Muffins with Bananas and Walnuts

makes about 1 dozen

The most popular fruit muffins? After a bit of research—both online and in my own cookbook library—I'd say it's a three-way toss-up between banana, blueberry, and apple (either applesauce or freshly chopped). I like to add crunch to the fruit muffins I make and old-fashioned rolled oats (oatmeal) does the job here. Ditto coarsely chopped walnuts. **Note:** *Make the topping first so it's ready to use as soon as the batter's in the pan.*

Topping:

¼ cup old-fashioned rolled oats (oatmeal)

1 tablespoon firmly packed light brown sugar

¼ teaspoon ground cinnamon

¼ teaspoon freshly grated nutmeg

1 tablespoon melted unsalted butter

Muffins:

1 cup sifted all-purpose flour

¼ cup firmly packed light brown sugar

2 teaspoons baking powder

½ teaspoon baking soda

½ teaspoon ground cinnamon

¼ teaspoon ground ginger

¼ teaspoon salt

1 cup old-fashioned rolled oats (oatmeal)

½ cup coarsely chopped walnuts

¾ cup buttermilk (not fat-free)

1 large egg

2 tablespoons melted unsalted butter

¾ cup mashed ripe bananas (about 2 small)

1 Preheat oven to 400°F. Lightly grease 12 standard-size muffin pan cups or spritz with nonstick cooking spray or, if you prefer, insert a crinkly muffin liner into each cup. Set pans aside.

2 **Topping:** Combine all ingredients in small bowl and set aside.

3 **Muffins:** Combine first seven ingredients (flour through salt) in medium mixing bowl. Add oats and walnuts, toss well, and make well in center of dry ingredients. Set aside.

4 Whisk buttermilk with egg and melted butter in second medium bowl until well blended, then mix in mashed bananas. Pour into well in dry ingredients, and stir only enough to mix. Specks of flour should be visible in batter.

5 Spoon batter into muffin pans, dividing amount equally—each muffin pan cup will be approximately two-thirds full, though occasionally a bit more or a bit less. Scatter topping over muffins, dividing amount evenly.

6 Slide onto middle oven shelf and bake 20 to 25 minutes until muffins have risen, their tops are gently rounded, and the topping lightly browned.

7 Serve at once with plenty of unsalted butter.

Honeyed Whole-Wheat English Muffins

makes about 8 muffins

The big-brand English muffins every supermarket carries today—believe it or not—were created in New York City at the turn of the twentieth century. The creator, however, was English, an immigrant named Samuel Bath Thomas who, according to food historian John Mariani (*Encyclopedia of American Food and Drink*), opened a bakery on Ninth Avenue in 1880 five years after arriving in New York. The recipe Thomas used for America's first commercial English muffins was his mother's. As with the basic recipe for English Muffins (page 69), I've turned this one into an easy oven one—no need to bake in batches on a griddle.

1½ cups sifted unbleached all-purpose flour

1 cup unsifted whole-wheat flour

¾ cup sifted bread flour

1¼ teaspoons salt

½ cup very warm water (105° to 115°F)

1 (¼-ounce) package active dry yeast

1 tablespoon honey

¾ cup milk, scalded and cooled to between 105° and 115°F

1 tablespoon yellow cornmeal (not stone-ground)

1 Whisk three flours and salt together in sturdy electric mixer bowl, insert mixing paddle, and set aside.

2 Place warm water in small bowl, add yeast and honey, stir until dissolved, then let stand uncovered until frothy—about 5 minutes.

3 Pour yeast mixture into mixer bowl, add warm milk, and beat until stiff dough forms, adding a bit more bread flour, if needed, or a little more milk. Remove mixing paddle, insert dough hook, and knead dough until supple and elastic—about 1 minute.

4 Turn dough into large buttered or oiled bowl, and turn buttered side up. Cover with wax paper, set in warm spot, and let rise until doubled in bulk—about 30 minutes.

5 Punch dough down, turn onto lightly floured surface, and knead gently about 1 minute. Shape into ball, return to buttered bowl, and again turn buttered side up. Cover with wax paper, set in warm spot, and let rise 30 minutes.

6 Meanwhile, lightly oil 8 muffin top pan cups or spritz with nonstick cooking spray and set aside. Sprinkle large sheet of wax paper with cornmeal and set aside also.

7 Punch dough down, knead gently until smooth. Divide dough into 8 balls and shape into burger-like patties about 3 inches across. Arrange, not touching, on cornmeal-sprinkled wax paper, then turn so both sides of each patty are lightly coated with cornmeal.

8 Set patties in muffin top cups, cover with wax paper, let rest 30 minutes. When muffins have rested 10 minutes, preheat oven to 400°F.

9 Slide muffins onto middle oven shelf and bake 5 minutes, then reduce oven temperature to 350°F and bake 15 minutes longer or until lightly browned.

10 Serve oven-hot with plenty of unsalted butter and/or jelly. Or, if you prefer, serve with a favorite honey—sourwood, perhaps, or tupelo—or just a delicate golden blend.

Fast & Flavorful
FRUIT
and/or
Nut Muffins

Of all the different types of muffins being made today—basic, cornmeal, whole-grain, and so forth—I have to say that fruit-and-nut muffins are my favorites.

Few muffins are more versatile or take better to improv than fruit and/or nut muffins—just substitute one nut for another, one dried fruit for another, or mix them up. You're home free as long as the total amounts remain the same. For example, if a particular recipe calls for ½ cup chopped pecans, why not ¼ cup each chopped pecans and toasted almonds? And instead of ⅔ cup raisins, why not ⅓ cup each raisins and dried cranberries or blueberries?

And here's another plus: These muffins stay fresh longer than plain muffins because the fruits they contain absorb and hold moisture. Moreover, they're great snack food and energy boosters. All of which make them ideal candidates for lunch boxes and picnic tables. And if baked as minis and pyramided on a silver platter, fruit-and-nut muffins are welcome on the fanciest tea table.

You'll find a variety of fruit-and-nut muffins in this chapter, some familiar, others not so familiar, and still others utterly unknown. Every one of them thoroughly tested.

Toasted Hazelnut Muffins anyone? Green Tomato Muffins? Spicy Chopped Apple Muffins? Fresh Pear–Pecan Muffins? Butternut–Pine Nut Muffins? Soy Flour Muffins with Dried Blueberries and Cranberries?

Try one, try all.

Toasted Hazelnut Muffins

makes about 1 dozen

I didn't acquire a taste for hazelnuts until I was quite grown up and had spent time abroad. Now I can't get enough of them and would choose toasted hazelnuts over pecans or walnuts. "Toasted" is the operative word here. Fortunately there's nothing difficult about toasting hazelnuts and the job can be done well ahead of time (see page 24). So how many whole hazelnuts equal ¾ cup coarsely chopped? Believe it or not, about ¾ cup, but to be on the safe side, I toast about 1 cup whole nuts, then chop and measure.

1¾ cups sifted all-purpose flour

2 tablespoons firmly packed light brown sugar

1 tablespoon baking powder

½ teaspoon salt

¾ cup moderately coarsely chopped toasted hazelnuts (see headnote)

¾ cup evaporated milk (not low-fat or fat-free) blended with ⅓ cup firmly packed chocolate-hazelnut spread

1 large egg

¼ cup vegetable oil or melted unsalted butter

1 Preheat oven to 400°F. Lightly grease 12 standard-size muffin pan cups, spritz with nonstick cooking spray, or insert a crinkly liner into each cup. Set pans aside.

2 Combine flour, sugar, baking powder, and salt in medium mixing bowl. Add hazelnuts, toss well, then make well in center of dry ingredients and set aside.

3 Whisk milk mixture with egg and oil in small bowl until smooth, pour into well in dry ingredients, and stir only enough to combine—specks of flour should be visible.

4 Spoon batter into muffin pans, dividing amount equally—each muffin pan cup will be approximately two-thirds full, though occasionally a bit more or a bit less.

5 Slide onto middle oven shelf and bake 20 to 25 minutes until muffins have risen and their tops are nicely rounded and evenly browned.

6 Serve warm with unsalted butter or, if you prefer, with chocolate-hazelnut spread.

Classic Carrot Muffins

The recipe my mother made when I was a little girl, these muffins are pretty much the ones many of us grew up on. I've trimmed the sugar somewhat but other than that, these muffins remain a favorite. If you'd like more of the crunchy tops (and what child doesn't?), try the muffin top variation at left.

2 cups sifted all-purpose flour

¼ cup firmly packed light brown sugar

1 tablespoon baking powder

1½ teaspoons ground cinnamon

½ teaspoon ground ginger

½ teaspoon ground allspice

½ teaspoon salt

½ cup coarsely chopped pecans or walnuts

½ cup dark seedless raisins or dried currants

1 cup milk

¼ cup vegetable oil

1 large egg

1 cup moderately coarsely grated tender young carrots (about 3 small)

1 Preheat oven to 400°F. Lightly grease 12 standard-size muffin pan cups, spritz with nonstick cooking spray, or insert a crinkly liner into each cup. Set pans aside.

2 Combine first seven ingredients (flour through salt) in medium mixing bowl. Add pecans and raisins, toss well, then make well in center of dry ingredients and set aside.

3 Whisk milk, oil, and egg in second medium bowl until smooth, then mix in carrots. Pour into well in dry ingredients, and stir only enough to combine—specks of flour should be visible in batter.

4 Spoon batter into muffin pans, dividing amount equally— each muffin pan cup will be approximately two-thirds full, though occasionally a bit more or a bit less.

5 Slide onto middle oven shelf and bake 20 to 25 minutes until muffins have risen and their tops are nicely rounded and evenly browned.

6 Serve oven-hot with plenty of unsalted butter or if you prefer, softened cream cheese. Good, too, with orange or ginger marmalade, Lemon Curd (page 214), or Maple Butter (page 216).

Green Tomato Muffins

Unlike ripe tomatoes, green tomatoes are usually available all year round (those rock-hard specimens barely blushed with pink can also be used). And their flavor is decidedly different—tart and, well, green. I like to turn them into muffins—great for breakfast with lots of butter, great for munching out of hand. **Note:** *To puree green tomatoes, core, chunk, and whiz in the food processor till smooth. No need to peel the tomatoes.*

2 cups sifted all-purpose flour

¼ cup loosely packed light brown sugar

2 teaspoons baking powder

½ teaspoon baking soda

½ teaspoon ground cinnamon

¼ teaspoon salt

⅓ cup coarsely chopped pecans

⅓ cup dried currants

¼ cup vegetable oil

1 large egg, well beaten with 1 tablespoon finely grated fresh ginger

1 cup pureed green tomatoes (about 2 medium) (see Note above)

1 Preheat oven to 400°F. Lightly grease 12 standard-size muffin pan cups or spritz with nonstick cooking spray or, if you prefer, insert a crinkly muffin liner into each cup. Set pans aside.

2 Combine first six ingredients (flour through salt) in medium mixing bowl. Add pecans and currants, toss well, then make well in center of dry ingredients and set aside.

3 Whisk oil and egg mixture in small bowl until smooth, then mix in pureed tomatoes. Pour into well in dry ingredients, and stir only enough to combine—specks of flour should be visible in batter.

4 Spoon batter into muffin pans, dividing amount equally—each muffin pan cup will be approximately two-thirds full, though occasionally a bit more or a bit less.

5 Slide onto middle oven shelf and bake 20 to 25 minutes until muffins have risen and their tops are nicely rounded and lightly browned.

6 Serve muffins oven-hot with unsalted butter or softened cream cheese. I also like these muffins with Maple Butter (page 216).

Spicy Chopped Apple Muffins

makes about 1 dozen

Choose apples that are crisp and tart for this recipe—Granny Smiths, Greenings, Staymans—because only they will impart deep apple flavor. And to point up that flavor, I add a little apple cider. **Note:** *If you cannot find apple pie spice, use ½ teaspoon ground cinnamon, ¼ teaspoon ground nutmeg, and ⅛ teaspoon each ground allspice and cardamom.*

2 cups sifted all-purpose flour

¼ cup granulated sugar or raw sugar

2 teaspoons baking powder

½ teaspoon baking soda

1 teaspoon apple pie spice (see Note above)

¼ teaspoon salt

½ cup moderately coarsely chopped pecans or walnuts

⅔ cup buttermilk (not fat-free) blended with ⅓ cup apple cider

1 large egg

¼ cup (½ stick) unsalted butter, melted

¾ cup moderately finely chopped peeled and cored tart apple (about 1 medium; see headnote)

1½ tablespoons Cinnamon-Sugar (page 217)

1 Preheat oven to 400°F. Lightly grease 12 standard-size muffin pan cups or spritz with nonstick cooking spray or, if you prefer, insert a crinkly muffin liner into each cup. Set pans aside.

2 Combine first six ingredients (flour through salt) in medium mixing bowl. Add pecans and toss well, then make well in center of dry ingredients and set aside.

3 Whisk buttermilk mixture with egg and butter in second medium bowl until well blended, then stir in apples. Pour into well in dry ingredients, and stir only enough to mix. Specks of flour should be visible in batter.

4 Spoon batter into muffin pans, dividing amount equally—each muffin pan cup will be approximately two-thirds full, though occasionally a bit more or a bit less. Scatter Cinnamon-Sugar evenly over unbaked muffins.

5 Slide onto middle oven shelf and bake 20 to 25 minutes until muffins have risen and their tops are gently rounded and lightly browned.

6 Serve at once with or without unsalted butter—these muffins really don't need butter.

Applesauce Muffins

makes about
1 dozen

The best applesauce to use is what you've made yourself but any good brand of bottled natural applesauce will do, "natural" meaning no added sugar or other sweetener or for that matter, anything other than apples, water, and ascorbic acid (vitamin C) to keep the applesauce from turning brown. I use very little sugar in this recipe because I don't like my muffins cupcake-sweet.

2 cups sifted all-purpose flour

2 tablespoons sugar

1 tablespoon baking powder

½ teaspoon ground cinnamon

¼ teaspoon ground allspice

¼ teaspoon freshly grated nutmeg

¼ teaspoon salt

1½ cups natural applesauce (see headnote)

¼ cup (½ stick) unsalted butter, melted

1 large egg, well beaten with 1 teaspoon finely grated orange or lemon zest

1 Preheat oven to 400°F. Lightly grease 12 standard-size muffin pan cups or spritz with nonstick cooking spray or, if you prefer, insert a crinkly muffin liner into each cup. Set pans aside.

2 Whisk first seven ingredients (flour through salt) together in medium mixing bowl, make well in center, and set aside.

3 Combine applesauce, butter, and egg mixture, beating until smooth, pour into well in dry ingredients, and stir only enough to mix. Specks of flour should be visible in batter.

4 Spoon batter into muffin pans, dividing amount equally—each muffin pan cup will be approximately two-thirds full, though occasionally a bit more or a bit less.

5 Slide onto middle oven shelf and bake 20 to 25 minutes until muffins have risen and their tops are gently rounded and lightly browned.

6 Serve at once with unsalted butter or Maple Butter (page 216).

VARIATION:

Extra Rich 'n' Spicy Applesauce Muffins: As soon as muffins come from oven, dip tops in ¼ cup melted unsalted butter, then in ¼ cup Cinnamon-Sugar (page 217).

EASY ADD-ONS (TOSS WITH DRY INGREDIENTS BEFORE ADDING COMBINED LIQUIDS):

* ½ cup coarsely chopped pecans or walnuts

* ½ cup dark seedless raisins or dried currants

* ½ cup dried blueberries

* ½ cup dried cranberries

Fresh Pear–Pecan Muffins

makes about 1 dozen

Choose pears with plenty of flavor when you make these muffins. My first choice: buttery Boscs, dead-ripe. Number two would be the intensely fruity, fine-fleshed Comices. Bartletts are more widely available, but when cooked, less flavorful. There are no spices in this recipe to mask the pears' delicate flavor, no vanilla or almond extract.

2 cups sifted all-purpose flour

½ cup sugar

2 teaspoons baking powder

½ teaspoon baking soda

¼ teaspoon salt

½ cup moderately coarsely chopped pecans

1 (8-ounce) carton (1 cup) sour cream

¼ cup milk

2 large eggs

1 cup finely diced peeled and cored pears (about 2 small or 1 large; see headnote)

1. Preheat oven to 400°F. Lightly grease 12 standard-size muffin pan cups or spritz with nonstick cooking spray or, if you prefer, insert a crinkly muffin liner into each cup. Set pans aside.

2. Combine first five ingredients (flour through salt) in medium mixing bowl. Add pecans, toss well, then make well in center of dry ingredients and set aside.

3. Whisk sour cream, milk, and eggs in small bowl until smooth, then mix in pears. Pour into well in dry ingredients, and stir only enough to combine—specks of flour should be visible in batter.

4. Spoon batter into muffin pans, dividing amount equally—each muffin pan cup will be approximately two-thirds full, though occasionally a bit more or a bit less.

5. Slide onto middle oven shelf and bake 20 to 25 minutes until muffins have risen and their tops are nicely rounded and evenly browned.

6. Serve oven-hot with plenty of unsalted butter.

Banana–Sweet Potato Muffins

makes about 1 dozen

Bananas and sweet potatoes go together like coffee and cream, especially when baked into muffins. These are the ones to make when you have leftover mashed sweet potato and a softening banana.

2 cups sifted all-purpose flour

¼ cup firmly packed light brown sugar

2 teaspoons baking powder

½ teaspoon baking soda

½ teaspoon ground cinnamon

¼ teaspoon ground ginger

¼ teaspoon ground allspice

½ cup moderately coarsely chopped pecans

¾ cup firmly packed mashed unseasoned baked sweet potato

⅓ cup firmly packed mashed ripe banana

¾ cup buttermilk (not fat-free)

¼ cup (½ stick) unsalted butter, melted

1 large egg, lightly beaten

1 Preheat oven to 400°F. Lightly grease 12 standard-size muffin pan cups or spritz with nonstick cooking spray or, if you prefer, insert a crinkly muffin liner into each cup. Set pans aside.

2 Whisk first seven ingredients (flour through allspice) together in medium mixing bowl. Add pecans and toss well, then make well in center of dry ingredients and set aside.

3 Combine sweet potato, banana, buttermilk, butter, and egg in second medium bowl, beating until smooth. Pour into well in dry ingredients, and stir only enough to combine—specks of flour should be visible in batter.

4 Spoon batter into muffin pans, dividing amount equally—each muffin pan cup will be approximately two-thirds full, though occasionally a bit more or a bit less.

5 Slide onto middle oven shelf and bake 20 to 25 minutes until muffins have risen and their tops are nicely rounded and lightly browned.

6 Serve muffins at once with plenty of unsalted butter. Good, too, at room temperature, even, a friend swears, leftovers right out of the refrigerator.

Pumpkin-Pecan Muffins

makes about 1 dozen

Have you noticed how sweet muffins are becoming? Does calling them muffins make us feel less guilty about eating them? These pumpkin muffins are definitely more muffin than cupcake.

2 cups sifted all-purpose flour

¼ cup raw sugar

1 tablespoon baking powder

1 teaspoon ground cinnamon

¼ teaspoon ground ginger

¼ teaspoon freshly grated nutmeg

¼ teaspoon salt

¾ cup coarsely chopped toasted pecans (see page 27)

1 cup milk

1 cup firmly packed canned pumpkin puree (not pumpkin pie mix)

1 large egg

¼ cup (½ stick) unsalted butter, melted, or ¼ cup vegetable oil

1 Preheat oven to 400°F. Lightly grease 12 standard-size muffin pan cups or spritz with nonstick cooking spray or, if you prefer, insert a crinkly muffin liner into each cup. Set pans aside.

2 Combine first seven ingredients (flour through salt) in medium mixing bowl. Add pecans and toss well to mix. Make well in center of dry ingredients and set aside.

3 Beat milk, pumpkin puree, egg, and butter in second medium bowl until well blended, pour into well in dry ingredients, and stir only enough to combine—specks of flour should be visible in batter.

4 Spoon batter into muffin pans, dividing amount equally— each muffin pan cup will be approximately two-thirds full, though occasionally a bit more or a bit less.

5 Slide onto middle oven shelf and bake 20 to 25 minutes until muffins have risen and their tops are nicely rounded and evenly browned.

6 Serve at once with unsalted butter or Maple Butter (page 216). Or, if you prefer, cool to room temperature before serving.

VARIATIONS:

Butternut-Blueberry Muffins: Prepare as directed, substituting ½ cup dried blueberries for pecans and 1 cup firmly packed, pureed, cooked butternut squash for pumpkin. Makes about 1 dozen.

Black Walnut–Sweet Potato Muffins: Prepare as directed, substituting ¾ cup coarsely chopped black walnuts (or English walnuts) for pecans and 1 cup firmly packed, mashed, cooked sweet potato for pumpkin. Makes about 1 dozen.

Butternut–Pine Nut Muffins

makes about 1 dozen

Instead of baking a butternut squash, scooping out and mashing the flesh, I've short-cut things by using frozen pureed winter squash—the unseasoned (package sizes vary from 9 to 12 ounces). You may have more squash than you need for this recipe. If so, just smooth the excess into a vegetable soup, pasta sauce, or gravy. Or mix into a casserole. **Note:** *For directions on how to toast pine nuts, see page 28. For ½ cup coarsely chopped toasted pine nuts, you'll need about ⅔ cup shelled nuts.*

2 cups sifted all-purpose flour

2 tablespoons firmly packed light brown sugar

¼ cup freshly grated Parmigiano-Reggiano or Pecorino Romano

1 tablespoon baking powder

½ teaspoon dried rosemary leaves, crumbled

¼ teaspoon salt

¼ teaspoon freshly ground black pepper

½ cup coarsely chopped lightly toasted pine nuts (see Note above)

1 cup firmly packed thawed frozen unseasoned butternut or winter squash

⅓ cup milk

¼ cup extra-virgin olive oil

1 large egg

2 tablespoons finely chopped untoasted pine nuts (topping)

1 Preheat oven to 400°F. Lightly grease 12 standard-size muffin pan cups or spritz with nonstick cooking spray or, if you prefer, insert a crinkly muffin liner into each cup. Set pans aside.

2 Combine first seven ingredients (flour through black pepper) in medium mixing bowl. Add toasted pine nuts, toss well, then make well in center of dry ingredients and set aside.

3 Whisk squash, milk, oil, and egg in second medium bowl until smooth, pour into well in dry ingredients, and stir only enough to combine—specks of flour should be clearly visible.

4 Spoon batter into muffin pans, dividing amount equally—each muffin pan cup will be approximately two-thirds full, though occasionally a bit more or a bit less. Sprinkle centers of muffins evenly with untoasted pine nuts.

5 Slide onto middle oven shelf and bake 20 to 25 minutes until muffins have risen and their tops are nicely rounded and lightly browned.

6 Serve muffins oven-hot with unsalted butter. Or set out little bowls of extra-virgin olive oil, then split the muffins, and dip just as you would with chunks of focaccia.

Sunrise Muffins

makes about 1 dozen

To be deeply flavorful, these orange muffins must be made with an orange on the tart side of sweet—Temples, for example, or Hamlins. I personally find Navels too sweet, too large, too *too*. But Mandarin oranges (a.k.a. tangerines) work well.

1 cup sifted all-purpose flour

1 cup unsifted whole-wheat flour

¼ cup granulated sugar or raw sugar

1 tablespoon baking powder

¼ teaspoon freshly grated nutmeg

¼ teaspoon salt

½ cup coarsely chopped dried cranberries

¼ cup freshly squeezed orange juice combined with 2 tablespoons tart orange marmalade

¼ cup (½ stick) unsalted butter, melted or ¼ cup vegetable oil

2 large eggs, lightly beaten

1 tablespoon coarse sugar crystals (optional topping)

1 Preheat oven to 400°F. Lightly grease 12 standard-size muffin pan cups or spritz with nonstick cooking spray or, if you prefer, insert a crinkly muffin liner into each cup. Set pans aside.

2 Combine first six ingredients (two flours through salt) in medium mixing bowl. Add cranberries, toss well, then make well in center of dry ingredients and set aside.

3 Whisk orange juice mixture, butter, and eggs in small bowl until smooth, pour into well in dry ingredients, and stir only enough to combine—specks of flour should be clearly visible in batter.

4 Spoon batter into muffin pans, dividing amount equally—each muffin pan cup will be approximately two-thirds full, though occasionally a bit more or a bit less—and, if you like, sprinkle coarse sugar lightly over each unbaked muffin.

5 Slide onto middle oven shelf and bake 20 to 25 minutes until muffins have risen and their tops are nicely rounded and lightly browned.

6 Serve muffins oven-hot with unsalted butter and/or orange marmalade.

Apricot Muffins with Toasted Almonds

makes about
1 dozen

Of all the dried fruits now available, dried apricots remain my favorite, maybe because my mother gave me a few to munch whenever between-meals hunger attacked. The recipe that follows is an old Southern one I found in my mother's card file of recipes.

1 cup dried apricots, moderately coarsely chopped

1 cup boiling water

2 cups sifted all-purpose flour

⅓ cup firmly packed light brown sugar

1 tablespoon baking powder

¼ teaspoon salt

½ cup coarsely chopped toasted slivered almonds (5 to 8 minutes in a 350°F oven)

1 cup milk

¼ cup (½ stick) unsalted butter, melted

1 large egg, lightly beaten with 1 teaspoon finely grated lemon zest

1 Preheat oven to 400°F. Lightly grease 12 standard-size muffin pan cups, spritz with nonstick cooking spray, or insert a crinkly liner into each cup. Set pans aside.

2 Soak apricots in boiling water in small bowl 5 minutes, drain well, and reserve.

3 Combine flour, sugar, baking powder, and salt in medium mixing bowl. Add almonds, toss well, then make well in center of dry ingredients and set aside.

4 Whisk milk, butter, and egg mixture in small bowl until frothy. Add drained apricots and mix well. Pour into well in dry ingredients and stir only enough to combine—specks of flour should be visible in batter.

5 Spoon batter into muffin pans, dividing amount equally—each muffin pan cup will be approximately two-thirds full, though occasionally a bit more or a bit less.

6 Slide onto middle oven shelf and bake 20 to 25 minutes until muffins have risen and their tops are nicely rounded and evenly browned.

7 Serve oven-hot with plenty of unsalted butter.

Holiday Muffins

Strewn with flecks of red (dried cranberries) and green (blanched pistachios), these muffins will brighten any breakfast or brunch throughout the long Christmas season. They are not very sweet and best served right out of the oven with butter and a favorite berry jam. I sometimes bake these as minis to serve at teas or open houses or just to eat as a snack (see variation that follows). **Note:** *To save time, use shelled and blanched pistachios—they're available online (see Sources, page 220).*

2 cups sifted all-purpose
flour

¼ cup sugar

1 tablespoon baking
powder

½ teaspoon salt

½ cup finely chopped
shelled and blanched
pistachios (see Note
above)

⅓ cup finely chopped
dried cranberries

1 cup milk

¼ cup (½ stick) unsalted
butter, melted, or
¼ cup vegetable oil

1 large egg, lightly beaten
with ¼ teaspoon finely
grated orange zest

1   Preheat oven to 400°F. Lightly grease 12 standard-size muffin pan cups or spritz with nonstick cooking spray or, if you prefer, insert a crinkly muffin liner into each cup. Set pans aside.

2   Combine flour, sugar, baking powder, and salt in medium mixing bowl. Add pistachios and cranberries and toss well to mix. Make well in center of dry ingredients and set aside.

3   Whisk milk with butter and egg mixture in small bowl until smooth, pour into well in dry ingredients, and stir only enough to combine—specks of flour should be clearly visible in batter.

4   Spoon batter into muffin pans, dividing amount equally—
    each muffin pan cup will be approximately two-thirds full,
    though occasionally a bit more or a bit less.

5   Slide onto middle oven shelf and bake 20 to 25 minutes
    until muffins have risen and their tops are nicely rounded
    and evenly browned.

6   Serve hot with plenty of unsalted butter and a favorite
    jam, preferably a red berry jam.

VARIATION:

Holiday Minis: Prepare step 1 as directed but instead of
using standard-size muffin pans spritz 30 mini muffin pan
cups with nonstick cooking spray or line with crinkly foil
cups. Proceed as directed in steps 2 through 5, but reduce
baking time to 10 to 12 minutes. Serve mini muffins whole
at room temperature or split, spread bottom halves with red
berry jam, replace tops, arrange on large platters, and serve.
Makes about $2\frac{1}{2}$ dozen mini muffins.

Soy Flour Muffins with Dried Blueberries and Cranberries

makes about 1 dozen

I wouldn't have thought of stirring soy flour into muffins until I received a press release from Linda Funk, executive director of The Soyfoods Council. After reviewing the impressive protein, iron, and calcium content of soy flour, I thought, what a good idea. So here's my own spin on the Soyfoods Council recipe. **Note:** *Some specialty groceries sell soy flour and it's also available online (see Sources, page 220).*

1¾ cups sifted all-purpose flour

½ cup unsifted natural or full-fat soy flour (see Note above)

½ cup sugar

1½ teaspoons baking powder

½ teaspoon baking soda

½ teaspoon salt

½ teaspoon freshly grated nutmeg

½ cup dried blueberries

½ cup dried cranberries

1 cup buttermilk (not fat-free)

¼ cup (½ stick) unsalted butter, melted

2 large eggs, lightly beaten with 2 teaspoons finely grated orange zest

1 Preheat oven to 375°F. Lightly grease 12 standard-size muffin pan cups, spritz with nonstick cooking spray, or insert a crinkly muffin liner into each cup. Set pans aside.

2 Whisk first seven ingredients (all-purpose flour through nutmeg) in large mixing bowl until well combined. Add blueberries and cranberries, toss well, make well in center of dry ingredients, and set aside.

3 Whisk buttermilk, butter, and egg mixture in small bowl until frothy, pour into well in dry ingredients, and stir only enough to combine—specks of flour should be visible in batter.

4 Spoon batter into muffin pans, dividing amount equally— each muffin pan cup will be approximately two-thirds full, though occasionally a bit more or a bit less.

5 Slide onto middle oven shelf and bake 20 to 25 minutes until muffins have risen and their tops are nicely rounded and lightly browned.

6 Serve hot with unsalted butter and a favorite jam or jelly.

Wild Persimmon Muffins

makes about 1 dozen

Until I worked as an assistant home demonstration agent in Iredell County, North Carolina, I never knew that wild persimmons, which proliferate over much of the South and Midwest, could be pureed (see page 27) and used in puddings, breads, and cookies. So why not muffins?

Note: *If wild persimmons are unavailable in your area, try the variation that follows, which substitutes pureed Fuyus (the big, sweet Japanese persimmons that most supermarkets sell) for the increasingly hard-to-find wild. The flavor and texture won't be quite the same, but the muffins will be very good. Frozen wild persimmon puree can sometimes be ordered online (see Sources, page 220) though you may be happier sweet-talking a friend, relative, or neighbor into selling you a pint or two. Also keep an eye out at local farmer's markets for baskets of fresh wild persimmons, which you can puree, yourself (see page 27). Even better, look for canned or frozen wild persimmon puree.*

2 cups sifted all-purpose flour

2 teaspoons baking powder

1 teaspoon ground cinnamon

½ teaspoon baking soda

½ teaspoon ground ginger

¼ teaspoon freshly grated nutmeg

¼ teaspoon salt

½ cup coarsely chopped pecans or walnuts

1¼ cups firmly packed unsweetened wild persimmon puree (see Note above)

¼ to ½ cup buttermilk (not fat-free) as needed to make a stiff but moist batter (see step 3 opposite)

¼ cup (½ stick) unsalted butter, melted

1 large egg, well beaten with 1 teaspoon finely grated orange or lemon zest

1 Preheat oven to 400°F. Lightly grease 12 standard-size muffin pan cups or spritz with nonstick cooking spray or, if you prefer, insert a crinkly muffin liner into each cup. Set pans aside.

2 Whisk first seven ingredients (flour through salt) together in medium mixing bowl. Add pecans, toss well, then make well in center of dry ingredients and set aside.

3 Combine persimmon puree, $\frac{1}{4}$ cup buttermilk, butter, and egg mixture in second medium bowl, pour into well in dry ingredients, and stir only enough to mix. If batter seems stiff and dry, mix in another $\frac{1}{4}$ cup buttermilk—batter should mound softly when you spoon it up. Try not to overmix—specks of flour should be visible in batter.

4 Spoon batter into muffin pans, dividing amount equally—each muffin pan cup will be approximately two-thirds full, though occasionally a bit more or a bit less.

5 Slide onto middle oven shelf and bake 20 to 25 minutes until muffins have risen and their tops are gently rounded and lightly browned.

6 Serve at once with or without unsalted butter.

VARIATIONS:

Fuyu Persimmon Muffins: Prepare as directed but eliminate buttermilk; Fuyu puree is more liquid than wild persimmon puree. Makes about 1 dozen.

Extra Rich 'n' Spicy Persimmon Muffins: As soon as muffins are done, dip tops in $\frac{1}{4}$ cup melted unsalted butter, then in $\frac{1}{4}$ cup Cinnamon-Sugar (page 217). Makes about 1 dozen.

More Muffin Recipes Containing Fruit and/or Nuts That Can Be Found Elsewhere in This Book

* Berry-Bran Muffins (page 127)

* Oat Muffins with Bananas and Walnuts (page 137)

* Black Walnut–Bran Muffins (page 129)

* Blueberry-Ginger Muffins (page 185)

* Old Vermont Cheddar–Cranberry Muffins (page 189)

* Blueberry Whole-Wheat Muffins (page 115)

* Brown Bread Muffins (page 133)

* Orange-Almond Muffins (page 51)

* Corn Muffins with Blue Cheese and Toasted Pecans (page 95)

* Orange Muffins (page 50)

* Date Muffins (page 36)

* Orange-Pecan Muffins (page 51)

* Date-Nut Muffins (page 36)

* Raisin-Bran Muffins (page 127)

* Fresh Strawberry Muffins (page 195)

* Raisin-Ginger Muffins (page 186)

* Green Mountain Apple Muffins (page 193)

* Thanksgiving Muffins (page 191)

* Maple-Nut Muffins (page 201)

* Upside-Down Pineapple-Carrot Muffins (page 123)

* Mississippi Muffins (page 183)

* Multi-Grain Muffins (page 118)

* Whole-Wheat Muffins with Black Walnuts (page 113)

* New England Blueberry Muffins with Maple Syrup (page 47)

* Not Your Mama's Carrot Muffins (page 121)

* Whole-Wheat Muffins with Dried Cranberries (page 113)

* Nut-Bran Muffins (page 127)

* Whole-Wheat Muffins with Raisins (page 113)

* Oatmeal-Applesauce Muffins (page 134)

Sweeter Muffins
for
BIRTHDAYS
&
Other Celebrations

When I lived on New York's Gramercy Park, the newsstand at the corner of Park Avenue South and Twenty-first Street sold the most delicious muffins—freshly baked, believe it or not, by some anonymous local baker.

The apple-cinnamon was my favorite with lemon–poppy seed running a close second. Both were jumbo-size, tender-crumbed, and as sweet as butter cake. If a swirl of frosting had been added, they'd have been sold as cupcakes.

When did muffins go cupcake-sweet? I have a hunch it may have happened after World War II; with sugar no longer rationed, we began binging on cakes and cookies and putting on the pounds. So to save a few calories, did we stop frosting our cupcakes, then to salve our guilty national conscience, begin calling them muffins?

Did we feel less guilty about eating something called muffins? Do we still? I knew full well that those apple-cinnamon muffins were as loaded with calories as the average cupcake, so every now and then I'd atone by switching to the raisin-bran muffins, telling myself that the bran nudged them into something approaching health food. Yeah, right. Those bran muffins were as big and sweet as the apple-cinnamon.

Because no muffin cookbook would be complete without a chapter on the richer, sweeter muffins so popular today, you'll find them in the pages that follow. I call them "party pleasers": Triple Lemon-Poppy Seed Muffins . . . Pennsylvania Dutch Buttermilk Muffins with Butter-Crumb Topping . . . Swirled Mocha Muffins . . . Green Mountain Apple Muffins . . . Sally Lunn Muffins . . . and, yes, even Chocolate Party Muffins.

Sally Lunn Muffins

makes about 1 dozen

This recipe comes from my good Chapel Hill friend, Mississippi-born-and-bred Moreton Neal, who's a superlative cook, facile writer, and ace interior decorator. Here's what she has to say about the muffins she used to bake as a teenager. "Must have been my grandmother's recipe. I remember having these muffins with lots of salted butter and molasses for breakfast, just like we put on biscuits. The molasses was made from cane and was quite tangy, not bitter like sorghum. I had some on waffles in Brookhaven, Mississippi, recently with the same local brand of cane molasses. It tasted just like I remember it did fifty years ago. Better than honey or syrup of any other kind. These can be served with a meal, too, just with butter. I don't know why they are called Sally Lunn since Sally Lunn bread usually has yeast, not baking powder. They should be eaten warm." **Note:** *The method of mixing is atypical, more like butter cake than muffins. No matter, the batter goes together fast and the muffins are in the oven in no time.*

1½ cups sifted all-purpose flour

1 tablespoon baking powder

⅓ cup salted butter, softened

⅓ cup sugar

1 large egg

⅔ cup milk

1 Preheat oven to 400°F. Lightly grease 12 standard-size muffin pan cups or spritz with nonstick cooking spray or, if you prefer, insert a crinkly muffin liner into each cup. Set pans aside.

2 Sift flour and baking powder onto piece of wax paper and set aside.

3 Cream butter, sugar, and egg 1 to 2 minutes in large electric mixer bowl at high speed until light and fluffy.

4 With mixer at low speed, add sifted dry ingredients to butter mixture alternately with milk, beginning and ending with dry.

5 Spoon batter into muffin pans, dividing batter equally—each muffin pan cup will be slightly less than two-thirds full.

6 Slide onto middle oven shelf and bake about 20 minutes until muffins have risen and their tops are gently rounded and lightly browned.

7 Serve at once with plenty of salted butter and cane molasses. It's the Mississippi way. I also think Lemon Curd (or Lime or Orange, page 214) superb on Sally Lunn Muffins.

Triple Lemon–Poppy Seed Muffins

makes about 1 dozen

The three lemon flavors? Freshly squeezed juice, freshly grated zest, and to round things out, freshly chopped lemon verbena, an exquisitely aromatic herb well worth growing. I keep a little pot of it—along with lemon geranium—in the garden window of my kitchen. **Note:** *Make sure that the poppy seeds you use are absolutely fresh.*

2 cups sifted all-purpose flour

½ cup granulated sugar

1 tablespoon baking powder

1 tablespoon poppy seeds (see Note above)

1 (5-ounce) can evaporated milk (not low-fat or fat-free)

¼ cup freshly squeezed lemon juice

¼ cup (½ stick) unsalted butter, melted

1 large egg, lightly beaten with 2 teaspoons finely grated lemon zest

2 tablespoons finely chopped fresh lemon verbena

1 tablespoon coarse sugar

1 Preheat oven to 400°F. Lightly grease 12 standard-size muffin pan cups, spritz with nonstick cooking spray, or insert a crinkly liner into each cup. Set pans aside.

2 Combine flour, sugar, and baking powder in medium mixing bowl. Add poppy seeds, toss well, then make well in center of dry ingredients and set aside.

3 Whisk milk, lemon juice, butter, and egg mixture in small bowl until smooth, then mix in lemon verbena. Pour into well in dry ingredients, and stir only enough to combine—specks of flour should be visible in batter.

4 Spoon batter into muffin pans, dividing amount equally—each muffin pan cup will be approximately two-thirds full, though occasionally a bit more or a bit less. Sprinkle each muffin lightly with coarse sugar.

5 Slide onto middle oven shelf and bake 20 to 25 minutes until muffins have risen and their tops are nicely rounded and evenly browned.

6 Serve oven-hot with plenty of unsalted butter or, if you prefer, Lemon Curd (page 214).

Pennsylvania Dutch Buttermilk Muffins with Butter-Crumb Topping

makes about 1 dozen

Years ago while writing a series of articles for *Family Circle* magazine called "America's Great Grass Roots Cooks," I interviewed Mary Rohrer, a superb Mennonite cook deep in Pennsylvania Dutch Country, and among her best recipes was a coffee crumb cake. I've reworked that recipe, deleted much of the sugar, and turned it into muffins that I have a hard time resisting. A friend and colleague who made them commented, "A good breakfast muffin, not too sweet." **Tip:** *It's best to make the topping first so it's ready to sprinkle over the muffins before they go into the oven.*

Topping:

½ cup sifted all-purpose flour

¼ cup firmly packed light brown sugar

¼ cup (½ stick) cold unsalted butter, diced (no substitute)

Muffins:

2 cups plus 2 tablespoons sifted all-purpose flour

½ cup firmly packed light brown sugar

2 teaspoons baking powder

½ teaspoon baking soda

½ teaspoon ground cinnamon

¼ teaspoon salt

1 cup buttermilk (not fat-free)

1 large egg

¼ cup (½ stick) unsalted butter, melted

1 Preheat oven to 375°F. Lightly grease 12 standard-size muffin pan cups or spritz with nonstick cooking spray or, if you prefer, insert a crinkly muffin liner into each cup. Set pans aside.

2 **Topping:** Whisk flour and sugar together in small bowl until well combined, then using pastry blender, cut in butter until mixture resembles coarse bread crumbs. Set aside.

3 **Muffins:** Combine first six ingredients (flour through salt) in medium mixing bowl, make well in center of dry ingredients, and set aside.

4 Whisk buttermilk with egg and butter in small bowl until frothy, pour into well in dry ingredients, and stir only enough to mix. Batter should be lumpy with specks of flour clearly visible.

5 Spoon batter into muffin pans, dividing amount equally—each muffin pan cup will be approximately two-thirds full, though occasionally a bit more or a bit less. Scatter topping over muffins, dividing amount evenly.

6 Slide onto middle oven shelf and bake about 25 minutes until muffins have risen, their tops are nicely rounded, and the topping is lightly browned.

7 Serve at once. Thanks to their buttery topping, these muffins don't need to be broken open and spread with additional butter.

Swirled Mocha Muffins

makes about
1 dozen

When I was a little girl, I loved making marble cake, dividing the yellow batter in half, coloring and flavoring one part with chocolate, then swirling the two together in the pan. Would the same technique work for muffins, especially if the sugar were reduced and instant espresso powder was substituted for some of the chocolate? Worth a try, I decided, and sure enough, muffin batter can be swirled as long as you don't overbeat and overswirl, either of which will toughen the muffins.

1 tablespoon instant espresso powder mixed with 1 tablespoon unsweetened cocoa powder

1⅓ cups milk

2 cups sifted all-purpose flour

⅔ cup sugar

1 tablespoon baking powder

¼ teaspoon salt

1 large egg

¼ cup (½ stick) unsalted butter, melted

2 teaspoons vanilla extract

1 Preheat oven to 400°F. Lightly grease 12 standard-size muffin pan cups or spritz with nonstick cooking spray or, if you prefer, insert a crinkly muffin liner into each cup. Set pans aside.

2 Whisk espresso mixture with 2 tablespoons of the milk in small bowl until smooth and set aside.

3 Combine flour, sugar, baking powder, and salt in medium mixing bowl, make well in center of dry ingredients, and set aside.

4 Whisk remaining milk with egg, butter, and vanilla in small bowl until smooth, pour into well in dry ingredients, and stir only enough to combine—batter should be lumpy with specks of flour clearly visible.

5 Eyeballing it, gently pour half of batter into second medium bowl and lightly fold in espresso mixture. It's critical at this point not to overbeat the batter because if you do, your muffins will be peaked and tough and riddled with tunnels.

6 Using ½ teaspoon measuring spoon, add 2 slightly rounded scoops light batter to a muffin pan cup, positioning at 12 and 6 o'clock. With second ½ teaspoon measuring spoon, add 2 lightly rounded scoops espresso batter to same muffin pan cup, this time at 9 and 3 o'clock. Add two more layers the same way reversing the colors each time—light on dark and dark on light.

7 Repeat until you have 12 muffins. Each muffin pan cup will be approximately two-thirds full, though occasionally a bit more or a bit less. Now with toothpick, gently swirl batter in each muffin pan cup. Easy does it.

8 Slide onto middle oven shelf and bake 20 to 25 minutes until muffins have risen and their tops are nicely rounded and lightly browned.

9 Serve at once with unsalted butter. Or to trim calories a bit, enjoy these muffins straight up.

Mississippi Muffins

I discovered these unusual muffins while researching my recent cookbook *From a Southern Oven*, and liked them so much I decided to reprint the recipe here. As I said in my original headnote, I have no idea why they're called Mississippi Muffins although I do know they're popular in this Gulf state and have, in fact, eaten them at the home of good Hattiesburg friends. Often baked as minis, these show up on Southern tea tables but I see no reason not to bake them full-size and serve at a child's birthday party or eat as a snack. The method of mixing here is more butter cake than muffin. No matter. It works well with these spicy "party pleasers." **Note:** *The best applesauce to use is what you've made yourself but any good brand of bottled natural applesauce will do, "natural" meaning no added sugar or other sweetener or, for that matter, anything other than apples, water, and ascorbic acid (vitamin C) to keep the applesauce from turning brown.*

2 cups sifted all-purpose flour

$\frac{3}{4}$ cup coarsely chopped pecans, walnuts, black walnuts, or hickory nuts

1 teaspoon baking soda

1 teaspoon ground cinnamon

$\frac{3}{4}$ teaspoon ground allspice

$\frac{1}{2}$ teaspoon ground ginger

$\frac{1}{2}$ teaspoon salt

$\frac{1}{4}$ teaspoon ground cloves

$\frac{1}{2}$ cup (1 stick) unsalted butter, slightly softened

1 cup granulated sugar

1 large egg

1 cup firmly packed applesauce (see Note above)

1 tablespoon confectioners' (10X) sugar (for dusting)

1 Preheat oven to 375°F. Lightly grease 12 standard-size muffin pan cups or spritz with nonstick cooking spray or, if you prefer, insert a crinkly muffin liner into each cup. Set pans aside.

2 Place ¼ cup flour and pecans in small bowl, toss to dredge, and set aside. Combine remaining 1¾ cups flour with next six ingredients (baking soda through cloves) by whisking in large mixing bowl and set aside also.

3 Cream butter in large electric mixer bowl at high speed 1 to 2 minutes until fluffy, add granulated sugar, and continue beating at high speed until almost white—about 2 minutes. Beat in egg.

4 With mixer at low speed, add combined dry ingredients alternately with applesauce, beginning and ending with dry and beating after each addition only enough to combine. By hand fold in pecans and all dredging flour.

5 Spoon batter into muffin pans, dividing amount equally—each muffin pan cup will be approximately two-thirds full, though occasionally a bit more or a bit less.

6 Slide onto middle oven shelf and bake 20 to 25 minutes until muffins have risen and their tops are nicely rounded and evenly browned.

7 Cool muffins in upright pans on wire racks 10 minutes, then remove from pans, turn muffins right side up, and cool to room temperature.

8 Sift confectioners' sugar over muffins until lightly dusted and serve. Nothing more needed.

VARIATION:

Mississippi Minis: Prepare step 1 as directed but instead of using standard-size muffin pans spritz 36 mini muffin pan cups with nonstick cooking spray or line with crinkly foil cups. Proceed as directed in steps 2 through 6 but reduce baking time to 13 to 15 minutes. To complete recipe, follow steps 7 and 8. Makes 2½ to 3 dozen mini muffins.

Blueberry-Ginger Muffins

makes about
1 dozen

When I was a little girl, my father grew blueberries on our lower lawn—a rarity then in North Carolina. Today, my home state is one of this country's major blueberry producers and I welcome spring when misty boxes of blues show up at farmer's markets. Off-season, I make do with frozen blueberries and, for baking, dried blueberries as well. Most supermarkets now routinely carry little packets of these alongside dried cranberries, currants, and raisins.

2 cups sifted all-purpose flour

¾ cup granulated sugar

1 teaspoon baking soda

½ teaspoon ground ginger

½ teaspoon ground cinnamon

½ teaspoon salt

½ to ¾ cup dried blueberries (see headnote)

1 cup buttermilk (not fat-free)

¼ cup (½ stick) unsalted butter, melted

2 tablespoons molasses (not too dark)

1 large egg, lightly beaten

1½ tablespoons Cinnamon-Sugar (page 217)

1　Preheat oven to 400°F. Lightly grease 12 standard-size muffin pan cups or spritz with nonstick cooking spray or, if you prefer, insert a crinkly muffin liner into each cup. Set pans aside.

2　Combine first six ingredients (flour through salt) in medium mixing bowl. Add dried blueberries, toss well, then make well in center of dried ingredients and set aside.

3　Whisk buttermilk, butter, molasses, and egg in small bowl until well blended, pour into well in dry ingredients, and stir only enough to combine—specks of flour should be visible in batter.

4　Spoon batter into muffin pans, dividing amount equally—each muffin pan cup will be approximately two-thirds full, though occasionally a bit more or a bit less. Then lightly sprinkle top of each muffin with Cinnamon-Sugar, dividing amount evenly.

5 Slide onto middle oven shelf and bake 20 to 25 minutes until muffins have risen and their tops are nicely rounded and evenly browned.

6 Serve warm or at room temperature with or without butter. I personally prefer these muffins as is—no butter.

VARIATIONS:

Cranberry-Ginger Muffins: Prepare as directed substituting coarsely chopped dried cranberries for dried blueberries. Makes about 1 dozen.

Raisin-Ginger Muffins: Prepare as directed substituting dark seedless raisins or, if you prefer, dried currants (in truth Zante raisins) for dried blueberries. Makes about 1 dozen.

Old Vermont Cheddar–Cranberry Muffins

makes about 1 dozen

This is my riff on an old recipe I picked up while in Vermont on article assignment more than twenty-five years ago. That recipe was for a fruit-nut bread, which I thought would make delicious muffins if a few adjustments were made. **Notes:** *If possible use granulated maple sugar in place of half the regular sugar. Also use the sharpest Cheddar you can find (see Sources, page 220).*

1 cup coarsely chopped fresh or solidly frozen cranberries or ⅔ cup dried cranberries

⅔ cup sugar (see Notes above)

2 cups sifted all-purpose flour

2½ teaspoons baking powder

¼ teaspoon baking soda

1 cup coarsely shredded sharp Vermont Cheddar (see Notes above)

¾ cup coarsely chopped walnuts, black walnuts, or pecans

½ cup freshly squeezed orange juice

2 tablespoons freshly squeezed lemon juice

1 teaspoon finely grated orange zest

1 teaspoon finely grated lemon zest

1 large egg, beaten until frothy

3 tablespoons vegetable oil or melted unsalted butter

1 Preheat oven to 400°F. Lightly grease 12 standard-size muffin pan cups or spritz with nonstick cooking spray or, if you prefer, insert a crinkly muffin liner into each cup. Set pans aside.

2 If using fresh or frozen cranberries, combine with ⅓ cup sugar in medium bowl and set aside 10 minutes. Whisk remaining ⅓ cup sugar with flour, baking powder, and baking soda in large mixing bowl. Add cheese and walnuts, and toss well. Make well in center of dry ingredients and set aside. **Note:** *If using dried cranberries, combine ⅔ cup sugar, flour, baking powder, and baking soda in large mixing bowl, add cheese, nuts, and dried cranberries, toss well to mix, then make well in middle of dry ingredients and set aside.*

3 Combine next six ingredients (orange juice through oil) in second medium bowl and when well blended, stir in fresh cranberry mixture (orange juice mixture if using dried cranberries). Pour into well in dry ingredients, and stir only enough to combine—specks of flour should be clearly visible.

4 Spoon batter into muffin pans, dividing amount equally—each muffin pan cup will be approximately two-thirds full, though occasionally a bit more or a bit less.

5 Slide onto middle oven shelf and bake 20 to 25 minutes until muffins have risen and their tops are nicely rounded and evenly browned.

6 Serve warm or at room temperature—no butter needed.

Thanksgiving Muffins

makes about 1 dozen

Two traditional Thanksgiving ingredients—cranberries and pumpkin—baked into muffins. I serve them right out of the oven with lots of unsalted butter and sometimes jellied cranberry sauce. Split the muffins, butter, then skim-coat with cranberry sauce. You can serve these muffins right around the calendar if you have frozen cranberries in the freezer. I always keep several bags of them there—for recipe testing and for enjoyment.

¾ cup fresh or solidly frozen cranberries, quartered or coarsely chopped

¾ cup sugar, raw sugar, or granulated maple sugar (see Sources, page 220)

2 cups sifted all-purpose flour

2½ teaspoons baking powder

½ teaspoon ground cinnamon

½ teaspoon ground ginger

¼ teaspoon baking soda

¼ teaspoon allspice

¼ teaspoon freshly grated nutmeg

¼ teaspoon salt

1 cup milk

½ cup firmly packed canned pumpkin puree (not pumpkin pie mix)

¼ cup (½ stick) unsalted butter, melted

1 large egg, well beaten with 1 teaspoon finely grated orange zest

1 Preheat oven to 400°F. Lightly grease 12 standard-size muffin pan cups or spritz with nonstick cooking spray or, if you prefer, insert a crinkly muffin liner into each cup. Set pans aside.

2 Combine cranberries with ¼ cup sugar in small bowl and set aside 10 minutes.

3 Whisk remaining ½ cup sugar with next eight ingredients (flour through salt) in large mixing bowl, then make well in center of dry ingredients and set aside.

4 Combine milk, pumpkin puree, butter, and egg mixture in medium bowl, beating until smooth. Mix in cranberry mixture, pour into well in dry ingredients, and stir only enough to combine—specks of flour should be clearly visible.

5 Spoon batter into muffin pans, dividing amount equally—each muffin pan cup will be approximately two-thirds full, though occasionally a bit more or a bit less.

6 Slide onto middle oven shelf and bake 20 to 25 minutes until muffins have risen and their tops are nicely rounded and lightly browned.

7 Serve muffins at once with plenty of unsalted butter and/or a jellied cranberry sauce.

Green Mountain Apple Muffins

makes about 1 dozen

Most apple muffins are so spicy you hardly taste the apples. But it shines through in this 100-and-something-year-old recipe given to me by my Sanford, North Carolina, friend Dea Martin. "The recipe," she emailed, "is from husband Thomas's Vermont great-grandmother Elva Buck and dates back to the late 1800s. I don't know what kind of apples she used," Dea continues, "but I use Galas and they are delicious." Like so many old family recipes, the one Dea sent had been written on an index card in a sort of shorthand. Almost cupcake-sweet, these are her favorite muffins. Added at the end of the original recipe—as a P.S. of sorts—is this note: "Batter may be refrigerated." I haven't tried this and don't recommend it because 1) the baking powder will lose much of its leavening power, and 2) any batter containing raw egg should be baked at once. **Note:** *The apple should be cored but not peeled—the red and yellow skins add color as well as texture.*

2 cups sifted all-purpose flour

1 cup sugar

1 tablespoon baking powder

1/2 teaspoon ground cinnamon

1/4 teaspoon salt

1 cup milk

1/4 cup (1/2 stick) unsalted butter, melted

1 large egg

1 cup finely diced, cored, unpeeled Gala apple (about 1 large; see Note above)

1. Preheat oven to 400°F. Lightly grease 12 standard-size muffin pan cups or spritz with nonstick cooking spray or, if you prefer, insert a crinkly muffin liner into each cup. Set pans aside.

2. Combine first five ingredients (flour through salt) in medium mixing bowl, make well in center of dry ingredients, and set aside.

3. Whisk milk, butter, and egg in small bowl until frothy, then mix in apple. Pour into well in dry ingredients, and stir only enough to combine—specks of flour should be visible in batter.

4. Spoon batter into muffin pans, dividing amount equally—each muffin pan cup will be approximately two-thirds full, though occasionally a bit more or a bit less.

5. Slide onto middle oven shelf and bake 20 to 25 minutes until muffins have risen and their tops are nicely rounded and evenly browned.

6. Serve oven-hot with plenty of unsalted butter or, if you prefer, apple butter (no butter needed). I also like these muffins with Maple Butter (page 216).

Fresh Strawberry Muffins

makes about 1 dozen

When I was a child, my father planted a strawberry bed—an acre, at least, it seemed to me back then because my jobs, and my brother's, were to keep that humongous bed weed-free, to separate the runners, and, of course, to pick the berries as they ripened. Mother was overwhelmed by the crop and tried her best to use up the annual gusher. She made strawberry shortcake (the biscuit kind), strawberry ice cream, strawberry jam, and even tried—unsuccessfully—to make strawberry muffins. I have only the vaguest memory of what went into those muffins and maybe that's just as well. Now I've taken up her cause and I think she'd be pleased with the results. **Note:** *Only red-ripe strawberries bursting with flavor will do for these muffins, so buy local. Even better, grow your own. You don't need a big patch of ground, something I wish my father had realized.*

8 ounces fresh strawberries, hulled, washed, and cut into ¼-inch dice (See Note above)

½ cup sugar

2 to 6 tablespoons freshly squeezed orange juice (depending on juiciness of strawberries)

2 cups sifted all-purpose flour

1 tablespoon baking powder

¼ teaspoon salt

⅓ cup melted unsalted butter or ⅓ cup vegetable oil

1 large egg

1 Mix strawberries and sugar in small bowl and set aside for 30 minutes. Strain berry mixture, catching juice in spouted glass measuring cup. Add enough orange juice to strawberry juice to total $^2/_3$ cup. Reserve diced berries.

2 Preheat oven to 375°F. Lightly grease 12 standard-size muffin pan cups or spritz with nonstick cooking spray or, if you prefer, insert a crinkly muffin liner into each cup. Set pans aside.

3 Combine flour, baking powder, and salt in medium mixing bowl, make well in center of dry ingredients, and set aside.

4 Whisk butter and egg in second medium bowl until frothy, then mix in strawberry juice mixture and diced strawberries. Pour into well in dry ingredients, and stir only enough to combine—specks of flour should be visible in batter.

5 Spoon batter into muffin pans, dividing amount equally—each muffin pan cup will be approximately two-thirds full, though occasionally a bit more or a bit less.

6 Slide onto middle oven shelf and bake 20 to 25 minutes until muffins have risen and their tops are nicely rounded and evenly browned.

7 Serve hot with plenty of unsalted butter or better yet, with Fresh Strawberry Butter (page 215). I may also put out a little jar of strawberry jam, sometimes in place of butter, sometimes in addition to it.

Note: *With Fresh Strawberry Butter, these muffins are equally good at room temperature.*

Chocolate Party Muffins

There's a magnificent food emporium called A Southern Season in the college town of Chapel Hill, North Carolina, that attracts shoppers from all over the South (and points north, too). Talk about one-stop shopping. You can get almost anything here—from freshly ground coffees to imported charcuterie and cheeses to every imaginable pot and pan and kitchen gadget. There's a popular restaurant, too, The Weathervane, where you can dine indoors or out, weather permitting. Among Chef Ryan Payne's recent offerings were oh-so-rich chocolate muffins drifted with mascarpone mousse. They were the inspiration for these not-quite-as-rich muffins, a good choice, I think, for any child's birthday party as well as for any picnic or potluck supper. And if baked as minis, these bite-size muffins are perfect for open houses and teas. Like many muffins made with less sugar and butter, these may dry on standing, so it's best to freeze any leftover muffins (not that you're likely to have any) and reheat just before serving (for directions, see page 15).

1³⁄₄ cups sifted all-purpose flour

¹⁄₄ cup unsweetened cocoa powder

¹⁄₂ cup raw sugar or light brown sugar (do not pack)

2 teaspoons baking powder

¹⁄₂ teaspoon baking soda

¹⁄₄ teaspoon salt

¹⁄₂ cup semisweet chocolate chips

1 cup buttermilk (not fat-free)

¹⁄₄ cup (¹⁄₂ stick) unsalted butter, melted

1 large egg, lightly beaten with 1¹⁄₂ teaspoons vanilla extract

1   Preheat oven to 400°F. Lightly grease 12 standard-size muffin pan cups or spritz with nonstick cooking spray or, if you prefer, insert a crinkly muffin liner into each cup. Set pans aside.

2   Combine first six ingredients (flour through salt) in medium mixing bowl. Add chocolate chips, toss well, then make well in center of dry ingredients and set aside.

3   Whisk buttermilk with butter and egg mixture in small bowl until frothy, pour into well in dry ingredients, and stir only enough to combine—specks of flour should be visible in batter.

4   Spoon batter into muffin pans, dividing amount equally—each muffin pan cup will be approximately two-thirds full, though occasionally a bit more or a bit less.

5   Slide onto middle oven shelf and bake 20 to 25 minutes until muffins have risen and their tops are nicely rounded and evenly browned.

6   Serve warm or at room temperature—no butter needed.

VARIATIONS:

Chocolate-Butterscotch Muffins: Prepare basic recipe as directed but substitute butterscotch chips for chocolate. Makes about 1 dozen.

Chocolate–Peanut Butter Muffins: Blend $\frac{1}{4}$ cup chunky peanut butter into buttermilk and substitute peanut butter chips for chocolate. Otherwise, prepare recipe as directed. Makes about 1 dozen.

Jumbo Muffins: The basic recipe and first two variations can be baked as jumbo muffins: Spritz 6 jumbo muffin pan cups with nonstick cooking spray, then proceed as directed but bake about 25 minutes. Serve at room temperature. Makes about 6 jumbo muffins.

Mini Muffins: The basic recipe and first two variations can be baked as mini muffins: Spritz 36 mini muffin pan cups with nonstick cooking spray or line with crinkly foil cups. Proceed as directed but reduce baking time to 10 to 12 minutes. Serve mini muffins whole at room temperature. Makes about 3 dozen mini muffins.

Maple-Nut Muffins

If these muffins are to have true maple flavor, you must use granulated maple sugar, pure maple syrup (preferably the more robust Grade B), and pure maple extract—the artificial are too "perfume-y." As for nuts, my first choice would be black walnuts because their slightly sweet, slightly musky flavor partners perfectly with maple. Second choice? English walnuts. And third? Pecans. But whichever nuts you choose, make sure they're absolutely fresh. **Note:** *If granulated maple sugar and pure maple syrup and extract are unavailable in your area, order them online. The same goes for black walnuts. See Sources (page 220).* **Tip:** *Prepare topping first so it's ready to scatter over the muffins just before they're baked.*

Topping:

¼ cup sifted all-purpose flour

¼ cup granulated maple sugar (see Note above)

2 tablespoons cold unsalted butter, diced (no substitute)

¼ cup moderately finely chopped black walnuts or English walnuts

Muffins:

2 cups sifted all-purpose flour

½ cup granulated maple sugar

1 tablespoon baking powder

¼ teaspoon salt

1 cup milk

1 large egg, lightly beaten with 2 tablespoons pure maple syrup and ½ teaspoon pure maple extract (see Note above)

¼ cup (½ stick) unsalted butter, melted (no substitute)

1 Preheat oven to 375°F. Lightly grease 12 standard-size muffin pan cups or spritz with nonstick cooking spray or, if you prefer, insert a crinkly muffin liner into each cup. Set pans aside.

2 **Topping:** Whisk flour and maple sugar together in small bowl until well combined. Using pastry blender, cut in butter until mixture resembles coarse bread crumbs. Add walnuts, toss well, and set aside.

3 **Muffins:** Combine flour, maple sugar, baking powder, and salt in medium mixing bowl, make well in center of dry ingredients, and set aside.

4 Whisk milk with egg mixture and butter in small bowl until smooth, pour into well in dry ingredients, and stir only enough to mix. Batter should be lumpy with specks of flour visible.

5 Spoon batter into muffin pans, dividing amount equally—each muffin pan cup will be approximately two-thirds full, though occasionally a bit more or a bit less. Scatter topping evenly over unbaked muffins.

6 Slide onto middle oven shelf and bake 20 to 25 minutes until muffins have risen, their tops are nicely rounded, and the topping is lightly browned.

7 Serve at once with plenty of Maple Butter (page 216).

SPREADS
& Toppings

Where is it written that muffins must be buttered like a biscuit fresh from the oven? First of all, not all muffins should be served while they're too hot to handle. Some are better served warm and in my opinion, many of the richer ones are best at room temperature.

As for butter, it's an option not a requirement. I've been eating muffins straight up for years but I've also been experimenting with spreads that may seem completely off-the-wall: Pimiento Cheese, even Hummus (nothing like them to dress up a plain muffin) ... Fresh Strawberry Butter (delicious on almost any plain muffin, whole-grain muffin, fruit-and-nut muffin) ... ditto Maple Butter and Lemon Curd.

Guacamole? Try it on corn muffins. Perfect. The same can be said for salsas mild or hot, even Pico de Gallo. Whenever company's coming, I like to put out all three so guests can choose whatever they fancy.

As I've said elsewhere, a frosted muffin is a cupcake. Not so a muffin sprinkled with Cinnamon-Sugar or Streusel (a buttery mix of sugar and flour and often nuts and spices, too).

The point of this chapter, then, is to share the many ways I like to jazz up muffins. Both before and after baking.

Pimiento Cheese

If you like pimiento cheese as much as Southerners do, it pays to keep it at-the-ready in the refrigerator. Most Southern supermarkets sell it, but I prefer to make my own—and not just for sandwiches. I often spread it on a favorite muffin instead of butter, and of course, it's terrific stuffed into celery or hollowed-out cherry tomatoes. **Tip:** *The fastest way to grate an onion is on a Microplane.* **Note:** *To save time, I often prepare pimiento cheese entirely by food processor—it's a snap if you have a sturdy model with an 11- to 14-cup bowl. Simply cut the cheese to fit the feed tube, pulse through the medium shredding disk, then tip onto a large piece of wax paper. Remove the shredding disk and insert the metal chopping blade. Next drop a 1-inch chunk of yellow onion into the work bowl and chop very fine. Add half the shredded cheese, all the other ingredients, then the remaining shredded cheese. Pulse just until the consistency of cream-style cottage cheese, pausing several times to scrape the work bowl. And there you have it: homemade pimiento cheese.*

1 pound very sharp
    bright orange
    Cheddar cheese,
    coarsely shredded

¾ cup firmly packed
    mayonnaise

3 (2-ounce) jars diced
    pimientos, well drained
    (reserve 3 to 4 table-
    spoons liquid)

2 tablespoons finely
    grated yellow onion
    (see Tip opposite)

2 tablespoons tomato
    ketchup

2 tablespoons reserved
    pimiento liquid (about)

1½ tablespoons milk or
    half-and-half

1 tablespoon prepared
    spicy brown mustard

¼ teaspoon freshly
    ground black pepper

1 Place all ingredients in large electric mixer bowl and beat at moderate speed for about 30 seconds or just until well blended. Mixture should be lumpy. If pimiento cheese seems too stiff to spread easily, add a little additional reserved pimiento liquid, tablespoon by tablespoon, until consistency of cream-style cottage cheese.

2 Transfer pimiento cheese to 1-quart plastic food container, press plastic food wrap flat on top, snap on lid, and allow to season in refrigerator overnight.

3 Use as a sandwich or muffin spread, as a stuffing for bite-size celery chunks or hollowed-out cherry tomatoes, or serve as a dip for crudités.

Note: *Stored tightly covered in the coldest part of the refrigerator, pimiento cheese will keep for 5 to 7 days.*

Guacamole

Firm-ripe avocados are the only ones to use for this recipe, meaning those that barely yield when you press them gently with your fingers. I'd also say that Hass avocados are a must because this California cultivar with pebbly dark purplish-black skin has an exquisite nutty flavor, which explains why it accounts for 80 percent of the annual U.S. crop. You should never feel guilty about eating avocados. They're superb sources of potassium, good sources, too, of vitamins A, C, and niacin (B_3). Moreover, avocados are low in sodium, cholesterol-free, and the fat they contain is largely unsaturated. Finally, one medium avocado weighs in at about 240 calories, some 50 fewer than a cup of whole-milk fruit yogurt. I often make this guacamole several hours, sometimes even a day or two in advance, and store tightly covered in the refrigerator. I've discovered that if I press a double thickness of plastic food wrap flat over the surface of the guacamole and into all the little valleys, then snap on a tight-fitting lid, it will not darken. Try spreading guacamole on corn muffins instead of butter. I think you'll like it. And if you should have any left over, serve later on with corn chips.

3 small firm-ripe Hass avocados (1¼ to 1½ pounds; see headnote)

2½ tablespoons freshly squeezed lime juice, or to taste

4 medium scallions, trimmed and finely chopped (include some green tops)

1 small garlic clove, finely minced

½ cup well drained, canned diced tomatoes with green chilies (as "mild" or "hot" as you like), patted dry on paper toweling

½ teaspoon salt, or to taste

½ cup loosely packed fresh cilantro leaves, washed, wrung dry in paper toweling, and coarsely chopped

1 Halve avocados, remove and discard pits, then scoop flesh into large nonreactive bowl. Sprinkle avocados with lime juice, then mash with potato masher—guacamole should be lumpy, about the consistency of large-curd cottage cheese.

2 Add all but final ingredient, taste for lime juice and salt, and adjust as needed. Fold in cilantro.

3 Scoop into 1-pint plastic food container, smooth plastic food wrap flat on top (see headnote), snap on lid, and store in refrigerator.

4 Stir guacamole well, scoop into a small bowl, and serve with freshly baked corn muffins.

Hummus (Sesame-Chickpea Spread)

makes about 2 cups

Before electric blenders, before food processors, this garlicky Middle Eastern sesame seed spread was the very devil to make. In Lebanon and Jordan I've seen women pound sesame seeds to paste (tahini) using large mortars and pestles—exhausting, tedious work. In that part of the world, hummus is ladled over falafel tucked into pita bread or spread on a variety of crisp flatbreads. I also like it spread on plain muffins in lieu of butter, particularly Toasted Benne Seed Muffins (page 52) and Falafel Muffin Tops (page 59). **Note:** *The tahini (sesame seed paste) you buy at your supermarket may have separated, leaving half an inch or so of oil floating on top and a thick tan paste underneath. No problem. Simply scoop everything into an electric blender or food processor and buzz for a minute or so—the tahini magically emulsifies. Once open, tahini should be refrigerated to keep it from turning rancid.* **Tip:** *To give hummus deeper sesame flavor, I add a little Asian toasted sesame oil, which most supermarkets now stock. Look for it in the "international" food section, the place where you'll also find tahini.*

1 (15½-ounce) can chick-
   peas, well drained and
   patted dry on paper
   toweling

2 large garlic cloves,
   smashed and skins
   removed

1 to 1½ teaspoons Asian
   toasted sesame oil,
   or to taste (see Tip
   opposite)

1 teaspoon salt, or to taste

¼ teaspoon freshly
   ground black pepper,
   or to taste

1 cup tahini (see Note
   opposite)

⅓ cup freshly squeezed
   lemon juice

¾ cup cold water (about)

3 tablespoons extra-virgin
   olive oil

1 Place first five ingredients (chickpeas through black pepper) in food processor and churn about 5 seconds until
   fairly smooth. Scrape work bowl sides down, add tahini
   and lemon juice, and pulse 4 to 5 times to incorporate.

2 With motor running, slowly drizzle water down feed tube
   until hummus is slightly softer than cream-style peanut
   butter, pausing once or twice to scrape down work bowl
   sides. Taste for salt, pepper, and sesame oil and adjust as
   needed.

3 Spoon hummus into small shallow bowl, cover with plastic
   food wrap, and refrigerate several hours or overnight.

4 About 1 hour before serving, set covered bowl of hummus
   on counter and bring to room temperature.

5 Remove plastic wrap and with bowl of large spoon, make
   shallow well in center of hummus, and add olive oil. Do
   not mix.

6 Serve hummus as a spread or dip for crisp triangles of pita
   bread, Arabic bread, or sesame crackers. Delicious, too,
   spread on fresh-baked muffins (see headnote), and as a dip
   for zucchini sticks, broccoli, and cauliflower florets.

Note: *Stored in a tightly capped container in the refrigerator,
hummus keeps well for about a week.*

Salsa

When tomatoes and fresh herbs are in season, salsa is a snap to make and handy to have on hand. Most of us ladle it into tacos. But why not muffins, especially corn muffins? Stored tightly covered in a nonreactive container in the refrigerator, salsa keeps well for about a week. **Note:** *The best tomatoes to use for this recipe are Romas or plum tomatoes because they have firmer flesh and fewer seeds.* **Tip:** *Over time the cilantro or parsley will darken, so add just before serving.*

1 pound medium-small plum tomatoes (6 to 8), moderately finely diced (see Note above)

¼ cup coarsely chopped red onion

2 large scallions, trimmed and moderately finely chopped (include some green tops)

1 medium jalapeño pepper, cored, seeded, and moderately finely chopped

1 to 2 tablespoons freshly squeezed lime juice, or to taste

Salt and freshly ground black pepper to taste

2 tablespoons coarsely chopped fresh cilantro or Italian (flat-leaf) parsley (see Tip above)

1 Place all but final ingredient (cilantro) in large nonreactive bowl and toss well to mix. Transfer to nonreactive container, cover tight, and store in refrigerator.

2 Before serving, let stand at room temperature 20 to 30 minutes—this brings out the flavors of the tomatoes and other ingredients—then fold in cilantro.

3 Serve with fresh-baked corn muffins instead of butter. It's a good way to trim calories, up the nutritional value, and add interest.

Pico de Gallo

Not for nothing is this Mexican salsa named Pico de Gallo ("Rooster's Beak"). It is fierce and sharp. "Liquid fire," a Santa Fe friend once called it, a condiment to be used sparingly. I've tamed the heat here and when I'm in a Southwestern mood, serve little bowls of this Pico de Gallo with a favorite corn bread or muffin. **Tip:** *Because the cilantro will darken, add shortly before serving.*

1 pound medium-small plum tomatoes (6 to 8), moderately finely diced

4 large scallions, trimmed and moderately finely chopped (include some green tops)

2 to 3 medium jalapeños, cored, seeded, and finely chopped depending on how "hot" you like things

1 medium garlic clove, finely minced

2 tablespoons freshly squeezed lime juice

½ teaspoon finely grated lime zest

½ teaspoon salt, or to taste

¼ cup coarsely chopped fresh cilantro, or to taste (see Tip above)

1 Place all ingredients except cilantro in large nonreactive bowl and toss well to mix. Transfer to 1-pint nonreactive container, cover tight, and store in refrigerator.

2 Remove from refrigerator, remove lid, and let stand at room temperature 20 to 30 minutes to "freshen" the flavors. Fold in cilantro.

3 Serve with corn muffins—good oven-hot, good at room temperature.

Note: *Stored tightly covered in a 1-pint glass preserving jar, pico de gallo keeps well for about a week.*

Lemon Curd

For centuries an English tea favorite, Lemon Curd (also called Lemon Cheese) was spread on scones or spooned into bite-size pastry shells. It still is—here as well as in Britain. Kept tightly capped in the refrigerator, lemon curd keeps well for several weeks. I find it particularly good with Sally Lunn Muffins (page 175), Blueberry-Ginger Muffins (page 185), indeed almost any plain muffin or fruit-nut muffin.

½ cup (1 stick) unsalted butter

1 cup sugar

⅓ cup freshly squeezed lemon juice

1½ tablespoons finely grated lemon zest

⅛ teaspoon salt

2 large eggs

1 Melt butter in top of small nonreactive double boiler over simmering water. Add sugar, lemon juice and zest, and salt, then cook and stir until sugar dissolves—2 to 3 minutes.

2 Beat eggs until frothy in small bowl, blend in ½ cup hot lemon mixture, stir back into pan, and cook, stirring constantly, until thickened—5 to 7 minutes.

3 Store in refrigerator in two tightly capped half-pint preserving jars and serve with muffins.

VARIATIONS:

Lime Curd: Prepare as directed but substitute fresh lime juice and zest for lemon. Makes about 2 cups.

Orange Curd: Prepare as directed but substitute freshly grated orange zest for lemon zest, but not orange juice for lemon juice. Makes about 2 cups.

Fresh Strawberry Butter

makes about 1 cup

When I lived in New York, I often trekked up to the old Mayflower Hotel on Central Park West to breakfast with friends. What brought us there was the fresh strawberry butter served with waffles and pancakes and almost every other bread right out of the oven. It's particularly good with muffins—basic ones, fruit-nut ones, or berry ones like Fresh Strawberry Muffins (page 195). **Note:** *The time to make this recipe is when local berries are in season and full of flavor. Settling for out-of-season berries shipped from farms thousands of miles away is a waste of time and money.*

1 cup (2 sticks) unsalted butter, at room temperature

4 large ripe strawberries, hulled, washed, halved, and patted dry on paper toweling (see Note above)

2 tablespoons honey (preferably a light golden one)

¼ teaspoon finely grated lemon zest (optional)

1 Place all ingredients in electric blender and whiz at high speed until smooth and fluffy. Pack into 1-cup decorative crock, cover, and refrigerate several hours or until firm.

2 Bring to room temperature before serving with freshly baked muffins (hot, warm, or at room temperature)—either the entire crock or some portion of it that's been scooped into a small bowl. Depends on how many you're serving.

3 Cover any leftover strawberry butter, refrigerate, and use within a day or so. Always bring to room temperature before serving.

Maple Butter

makes about
1½ cups

Just the thing for Maple-Nut Muffins (page 201), but equally delicious on almost any muffin (other than corn muffins), pancake, or waffle. *Note: This recipe, unlike the majority in this book, calls for salted butter and here's why. If you try to beat a small amount of salt into this butter, even as little as ⅛ teaspoon, the salt crystals do not dissolve, leaving it unpleasantly gritty.* **Tip:** *I prefer Grade B maple syrup, which has more pronounced maple flavor than Grade A (see Sources, page 220).*

1 cup (2 sticks) salted
  butter, at room
  temperature (see
  Note above)

¼ cup pure maple syrup
  (see Tip above)

1 Beat butter in small electric mixer bowl at high speed until smooth and fluffy.

2 Reduce mixer speed to low and drizzle maple syrup into whipped butter. Continue beating at moderate speed until absolutely smooth.

3 Scoop into small decorative bowl or crock and serve with freshly baked muffins—hot, warm, or at room temperature. Or serve with waffles or pancakes hot off the griddle.

4 Cover any leftover maple butter, refrigerate, and use within a day or so. Always bring to room temperature before serving.

Cinnamon-Sugar

makes 1 cup

I like to keep a batch of Cinnamon-Sugar on hand not only for cinnamon toast but also for mixing into baked goods or sprinkling on top of them—cookies, fruit-nut loaves, muffins, and so forth. I store Cinnamon-Sugar in a tightly capped half-pint preserving jar on my shelf of herbs and spices. It seems to keep forever. **Note:** *Make sure the cinnamon you buy is a good one—a brand you know and trust. Believe it or not, there are several varieties of cinnamon out there, the two most popular being cassia (Chinese cinnamon) and true cinnamon (also known as Ceylon cinnamon), and that's the one to use here. It's less sweet than cassia and has the assertive spicy flavor that's best for baking.*

1 cup sugar

2 tablespoons ground cinnamon (see Note above)

1 Place sugar and cinnamon in small bowl and stir until well blended.

2 Transfer to half-pint preserving jar, screw lid down tight, and set on cool, dark shelf.

3 Use whenever a recipe calls for Cinnamon-Sugar. For a final flourish, I sometimes sprinkle a little Cinnamon-Sugar on top of fruit and/or nut muffins just before I slide them into the oven.

Streusel

Streusel is German for "scattered" or "sprinkled," which is exactly what you do with these crumbly toppings. They not only dress up a variety of baked fruit desserts but many a muffin, too. I like streusel best on whole-grain or fruit-nut muffins (plenty of both in this book) and keep a plastic zipper bag of it ready and waiting in the freezer. It keeps well for about six months. **Note:** *Whenever I top muffins with streusel, I bake them at 375°F to minimize the risk of over-browning the rich, buttery streusel. So if the baking temperature of the muffins you plan to top with streusel is 400°F, reduce it to 375°F, bake the muffins a few minutes longer, and test for doneness as directed below.*

1 cup sifted all-purpose flour

⅔ cup firmly packed light brown sugar

6 tablespoons cold unsalted butter, diced (no substitute)

¼ teaspoon salt

1 Pulse all ingredients in food processor until texture of coarse meal.

2 Scoop streusel into medium plastic zipper bag, seal, and set in freezer.

3 When ready to use, sprinkle about 1 teaspoon streusel on top of each muffin just before you slide pan into oven. Streusel browns fairly fast, so as soon as a toothpick inserted in center of muffin comes out clean, remove muffins from oven.

4 Serve muffins hot or at room temperature with or without unsalted butter and/or jam.

VARIATIONS:

Spicy Streusel: Prepare as directed but add 1 teaspoon ground cinnamon and $\frac{1}{2}$ teaspoon each ground ginger and freshly grated nutmeg. Makes $1\frac{1}{2}$ to 2 cups.

Nut Streusel: Prepare as directed, then mix in $\frac{1}{2}$ cup moderately finely chopped pecans or walnuts. Makes about 2 cups.

SOURCES

Bacon (*slab*):
www.flyingpigsfarm.com
www.nueskes.com

Black walnuts (*shelled and ready-to-use*):
www.earthy.com
www.hammonsproducts.com

Cornmeal (*stone-ground*):
www.ansonmills.com
www.oldmillofguilford.com

Corn powder (*freeze-dried*):
www.shopmilkbar.com/shipping.shop/
corn-powder

Country ham:
www.newsomscountryham.com
(small amounts available)
www.edwardsvaham.com (ham slices available)
Note: *Ham must be fully cooked.*

Hickory nuts (*shelled and ready-to-use*):
www.rayshickorynuts.com
www.hickorynutsfarm.com

Maple extract (*pure*):
www.olivenation.com
www.cooksvanilla.com
www.kitchenkapers.com

Maple sugar (*granulated*):
www.vermontpuremaple.com
www.vermontcountrystore.com
www.sugarbushfarm.com

Maple syrup (*Grade B*):
www.maplesyrupworld.com/pages/
Where-to-Buy-Grade-B-Maple-Syrup
www.piecesofvermont.com
www.vermontcountrystore.com
www.vermontpuremaplesyrup.com

Masa harina:
www.bobsredmill.com
www.myspicesage.com/masa-harina-p-1279.html

Muffin pans (*and almost everything else you need to make muffins*):
www.kitchenworksinc.com
www.chefscatalog.com
www.williams-sonoma.com
www.wilton.com

Pecans:
www.doubletreepecan.com
www.pearsonfarm.com
www.surrattfarms.com

Pico de gallo, salsas:
www.mexgrocer.com (Sandra Gutierrez, cookbook author and my go-to source for Latino foods, says that Herdez brand Salsa Casera "is a great pico de gallo." Many other salsas available here, too.)
www.madeinnewmexico.com/salsas.html
www.tastenewmexico.com/our-products

Pistachios (*blanched, unsalted, raw or roasted*):
www.nuts.com

Rye flour:
www.arrowheadmills.com
www.bobsredmill.com
www.kingarthurflour.com

Sausage meat (*bulk*):
www.georgiacountrysausage.com
www.newsomscountryham.com

Soy flour:
www.hodgsonmillstore.com/en/flours-and-meals/
www.nuts.com/cookingbaking/beans/soybeans/
flour.html
www.vitacost.com

Vermont Cheddar:
www.igourmet.com
www.vermontcountrystore.com

Whole-wheat flour:
www.arrowheadmills.com
www.kingarthurflour.com

Wild persimmon puree (*usually available only in fall and early winter*):
www.persimmonpudding.com/sources.html

INDEX

Note: Page references in *italics* indicate photographs.
Page references in **bold** indicate recipe variations.